A CUP OF COMFORT®

for

Divorced Women

Inspiring stories
of strength, hope,
and independence

Edited by Colleen Sell

A **adams**media
Avon, Massachusetts

For Nikk, who patiently and tenderly convinced me that
true love and true partnership really do come true.

Published by
Adams Media, an F+W Media Company
57 Littlefield Street, Avon, MA 02322 U.S.A.
www.adamsmedia.com and *www.cupofcomfort.com*

ISBN 10: 1-59869-652-1
ISBN 13: 978-1-59869-652-3
Printed in the United States of America.

J I H G F E D C B A

Library of Congress Cataloging-in-Publication Data
is available from the publisher.

This book is available at quantity discounts for bulk purchases.
For information, please call 1-800-289-0963.

Contents

Acknowledgments

To my children, who paid the dearest price for my marital mistakes, to my ex-husbands, and to the many divorced women in my life I owe a huge debt of gratitude. Without the experiences each has shared with me, I would not have had the understanding to recognize which of the more than 2,000 stories received for this book would bring the most comfort to women who are considering, in the throes of, or recovering from divorce.

To the women who have shared their stories in these pages, bravo! And my deep appreciation.

To the stellar team at Adams Media—especially Meredith O'Hayre and Laura Daly—a tip of the hat for another job well done. You give new meaning to the words talent and teamwork.

Introduction

"*Losing is the price we pay for living. It is also the source of much of our growth and gain.*"

—Judith Viorst

It is often said that divorce is like a death. Having mourned the losses of two marriages, I can attest that it does feel very much like the death of a loved one. But divorce is not death. Life goes on. And it gets better in time. Divorce is an ending, yes, but it is also a beginning.

But when you're in the last hours of a dying marriage, in the throes of divorce, and in the grieving period that follows, it can be difficult to see the light at the end of that long, dark, lonely, scary tunnel. Most about-to-be and newly divorced women wonder, as I certainly did, *Am I doing the right thing? How will I survive? Will my children and I ever be okay again? Are my home and my heart broken beyond repair? Do the guilt and shame and pain ever go away?*

Fortunately, women often turn to those who've walked in our shoes and listen raptly to their tales of survival and healing and rebirth. When we are too numb with grief to ask for help, it often comes to us unbidden in the caring words of friends offering up their personal stories of trial and triumph. These stories give us insight, hope, and strength. They tell us that we are not alone in that tunnel, that it isn't as long and scary as it seems, and that there is light ahead. And if you move steadily toward that light, following in the direction of the women who've gone before you, you will find at the end of that tunnel a brilliant new life of your own making.

The illuminating stories in *A Cup of Comfort®️ for Divorced Women* shed the restorative light of understanding on divorce from a woman's point of view. These personal stories reveal the universal truths that only women who have been through and moved beyond a divorce can know: That time, properly spent, does heal all wounds. That there really are two sides to every breakup, and neither is completely right nor completely wrong. That you can rise above and beyond the devastation. That you can, indeed, grow and gain from divorce.

—Colleen Sell

On the Road to Redemption

Coastal Mexico's road from Puerto Vallarta inland to Mascota is sweet. It winds for a breathtaking ninety minutes through the velvety Green Mountains. Driving it, you can get into a rhythm like dancing: looking ahead, judging the curve, letting the arm muscles make just enough effort to take the inside and ease back over. It's a great game to never use the brakes to slow down, just the motor, downshifting. Once I followed a high-tailing, rusty pickup I thought had no brake lights until the very last switchback, when he lost the zone (thoughts of dinner?) and they flashed on. Driving with skill on these mountain roads is fun, and it makes you thank God you have a car.

But most times now when I make that trip, I take the 3:30 bus out of Vallarta. It's a rickety, old, beat-up blue thing with no suspension left, and the windows don't shut, so the wind whistles, but I've learned to like it fine.

You see, in the car, there's only one story—mine. On the bus, there are other stories, not sad like mine, but often happy and brave stories, in spite of the fact that the other people who take the blue bus certainly would take their car if they had a car. But they are too poor and thank God for their shoes, instead. Unfortunately, for me, these stories are in Spanish—and not even recognizable Castilian, but the drawled Spanish of country people. And with the wind whistling and with my aging, failing ears popping from the altitude changes as we ascend and descend, I have to guess at the plot lines. But never at the characters; they are always large and clear.

Riding the bus also requires some give and take. Still, I do my part, even speaking Spanish like a young child. I held the hand of a girl going home to her village to tell her parents the bad news. It took few words to read that old story in her beautiful, tear-filled eyes, hardly any words at all to say they would still love her, of course they would.

A country woman gave me valuable plant advice, which I struggled to understand but finally got it. "Save the egg shells in water, crush them up, and give them to your plants. Get the best dirt for your plants by the river, where it is rich and black—and free!" An easy place, she told me, is "the flat spot where the road crosses the river in Mascota, where people wash their cars, don't you know, close to Ángel's, with the horses, whose one eye goes off. You know, Ángel, don't you? *Señora*, get your dirt by Ángel's and your geraniums will have leaves like emeralds!" You can see how I could have gotten the plot wrong there, but finally I sorted the "eye" out from the "emeralds," and understood.

These are things women must know, and I can learn them on the bus. These are the things we do for each other. So it is that love is given and taken.

But what happened on my last bus trip was the best of all. Let me tell you.

At the stop in Ixtapa, where the workers who service Vallarta live in humble casitas, an elderly couple climbed aboard, laden with shopping bags.

"Mascota?" the driver inquired.

"Sí," the woman answered him with a friendly, gap-toothed grin.

I shifted my things and made room for her with me in the bigger front seat by the door. I'd been persistent enough to snag it for my long legs, the prize among bus seats. Her husband took the high-perched rumble seat by the driver. I knew he was her husband by the way he had helped her on the bus, with a boost to her generous rump that he followed with a husbandly little pat. Both turned as the bus was pulling away and waved at a group of locals waving back at them—two young women standing arm-in-arm in a storefront, who blew kisses; a whole family from a dusty park bench; a young man on a bicycle; and an older man on horseback on the road. Ixtapa bid them farewell, waving affectionately long after we pulled away. She settled back in the seat and sighed contentedly. Her husband, a slim man with a smiling elfin face and full head of curly hair despite his obvious years, paid their fare and struck up pleasantries with the driver.

She had the skin problem that takes away the pigmentation in patches, but her face was so frank and friendly, a stranger would notice the discoloration only at the first glance. At first glance, you would see a plump old woman in her seventies, at least, with wind-tousled, grey-streaked hair, wearing a cheap white skirt a little soiled with road dust and peppered with what appears to be cake crumbs, disintegrating cloth Mary Jane shoes, and torn stockings. You would see she wore her rosary around her neck in the way of people here and carried a cheap, pink, plastic purse. And that her olive skin was covered with beige patches. But only at the first glance. Then, you would forget all that. You would look into her sparkling brown eyes and see—mischief! You would see liveliness, compassion, intelligence, and not a shadow of grief.

Soon, of course, we were deep in conversation. I have no shame about my Spanish, although I should have. She had a country woman's slow speech, which I could understand. We talked about the road, the weather, cooking. We talked about her family. Eleven children, she said with calm satisfaction, six boys, five girls. She named each one for me. This took some time.

"Are they here," I asked, "or there?" Many families now are split by the border, and houses stand empty or are populated only by the women and children left behind. "All here," she told me with a smile. "Were you visiting them in Ixtapa?" I asked. "No, just friends," she smiled again. "Like you," she added kindly and actually patted my cheek.

Every few minutes during our conversation her husband in the rumble seat by the driver would rummage in a shopping bag to offer her a sweet or water, and she would lean out across the aisle and take it without regard for the undignified position of her rear. He gave her a little bag of candy-coated peanuts, then a cellophane bag of jellied candies, and finally a bag of popcorn. Each time, they exchanged an affectionate smile. She offered me some, of course; and, of course, I said no thanks, and considered delivering my carbohydrates lecture. But if there ever was a person about whom I thought it really might not matter, it was her. What difference does it make, as long as you had someone to smile at you like that? When your rump was a little oversized but lovingly patted?

Then it was my turn in the conversation to talk about family. I named my three sons and how one's wife is from Russia, how another is struggling with alcohol addiction, and how the one who was toughest to parent as a teen is turning out to be a wonderful man.

Then she had to ask me about my husband. I'd volunteer almost anything personal but never about the husband who wasn't there. I'd never volunteer the information that the husband had "changed addresses." If I put it that way I can manage not to cry for at least two minutes, and sometimes the conversation will take a turn and I'm safe.

But this conversation took a most surprising turn—it stopped altogether! She leaned back in her seat and closed her eyes and appeared to go to sleep. Except that she began to strike things. She smacked a fist into her hand. She slapped her knee. She pulled her hair. She kicked the barrier in front of the seat, and then began the sequence all over again. I was quite puzzled. I began to think I had met the physical equivalent of Tourette's syndrome, for she seemed unconscious of her movements and they had no apparent relation to our conversation. It was mystifying. Perhaps I had said something other than what I thought I said? It happens with my Spanish.

Suddenly, she sat upright and leaned close to my ear. "How many years?" she whispered.

"I'm sixty-one," I whispered back.

"No, no. How many years was your marriage?"

"Oh. Twenty-seven," I said sadly.

I knew for sure my tears were going to come then, darn it. *I'd rather run a marathon than have this conversation*, I thought, preparing to feel emotionally exhausted, as usual. But she interrupted my thoughts by smacking her thigh smartly, and then I realized: She was angry. She was really angry. She was angry for me!

What a shock! It sure hadn't been like that at home.

My own best friend back in the states hadn't been angry when I told her the news that my husband had stood in our kitchen and said as casually as if he were reporting a car problem, "Oh, by the way, I've made us an appointment for mediation next Monday. I've met someone, and I'm moving out. Mediation's the cheapest way to go." My best friend asked me not to make her choose sides and refused to discuss it further.

The counselor I found in the phone book shared that she was planning her own divorce and advised me that divorce was perfectly normal, people had to grow, had to move on. The neighbors looked discreetly away. My employer didn't want any tears on the job; they just wanted their cool, calm, collected, and competent teacher, as always. Somebody at school told the students it was important to be neutral. Nobody wanted to hear that it hurt. If it hurt, I had "abandonment issues," not a divorce problem.

In my poetry group, a thirty-something woman with two daughters, ages three and five, discussed leaving her husband to improve her poetry. No one argued with her basic premise: The girls will be happy if I'm happy. No one argued that the attitude of "me first" does not even make for very good poetry.

The very first thing my own divorce lawyer told me, when I was finally able to get one to call me back in the evening so I wouldn't miss work, was, "I am not a vindictive person, so if you want someone to 'get him' for you, you need another lawyer." Then, in the property settlement, she let him have the whole business (we both had borrowed for it), under his lawyer's argument that it wouldn't run without his labor and thus was of zero worth, nothing to be shared. As soon as we signed the property settlement, he sold the machinery my polite lawyer had thus overlooked as an asset, giving me not a dime of the profit, while I was left with my "fair share" of the debt we had incurred to buy it. Welcome to the new no-fault. The new feminism. Nobody's supposed to get mad or get even. This is divorce, twenty-first century American style.

And here was a stranger getting mad enough to smack herself over it. Getting so angry she ruined her heretofore happy day. What nobody in my hometown would do for me and what I didn't even know I needed. Here it was, falling like sunshine on me in a bouncing bus on a dusty mountain road in the middle of Mexico.

Suddenly, I didn't feel like crying. Something had shifted inside me, like a bone in its socket. I felt pretty good, all things considered. "There, there," I murmured, patting the place on her leg where she had hit herself with her little, fat, bi-colored fist. "Don't be upset," I said to her. "I can bear it."

We had not much farther to go to descend into the Mascota Valley and reach the terminal. We exchanged names—Concepción is hers. She gave me explicit directions to her house from the terminal, but I have a feeling I won't have any trouble finding her. I think everyone in Mascota must know Concepción. I wouldn't be surprised if she had a shingle over her doorway that reads "Healing Here Tonight." I'm going to visit.

—*Janet Baker Hayhurst*

Can't Stop the Ocean

"Why are you stealing Papa's money?" asked my three-year-old son as I helped him out of the car.

Even today, eight years later, I could pinpoint that parking space, show where the sun had been in the sky as it curved over his round cheeks. Ben's arms were folded across his chest, and his brow furrowed with accusation and anger.

No! I thought. *Please. Don't let this be the start of how things are going to be.*

But it was.

My husband and I had separated just a few weeks before. We had talked about the importance of protecting Ben and his baby sister, Charlotte. But the desire to do the right thing was apparently only one of the forces at work in his mind. Other needs were stronger.

In that instant in the parking lot, I felt a help-lessness I had never known before. I could not make Allan stop, nor could I separate him from Ben. I was watching a terrible accident beginning to take place, knowing exactly what would happen and how and being unable to do the slightest thing to stop it.

On the spot, I said that maybe Papa had misun-derstood or maybe Papa was confused. Papa and I had a few disagreements about who owned what, I explained. But there was no stealing involved; just different ideas of what belonged to whom.

Ben seemed to understand.

The next time he came back from his father's, though, he had a different explanation.

"You're stealing Papa's money and you're lying about it," he said.

Without children, I could have divorced and moved on to discover and create my own new hori-zons. Instead, I saw before me a hostage situation that would probably persist, in one form or another, for the next seventeen years. I couldn't solve it. And I now knew that my ex-husband would say one thing to me and something else to my children, and then deny it all. I had not known that about him.

This conflict was so far from the perfect world we'd hoped to create for our children that I was stunned into inaction. When we'd set out to have children, we were determined to make everything as perfect for them as we possibly could. We read all the recommended books and bought all the necessary equipment, after double-checking with *Consumer Reports* for the latest safety information. And I prepared for what I thought best: a medication-free birth.

The technique I used is called the Bradley technique, and there's deceptively little to it. Visualize each contraction as a wave. Soften into it, let it go right through you, and then rest until the next one. Slowly, unobtrusively, underneath all the flinging advances and apparent retreats, the waves claim more of the shore and eventually bring your baby into your arms. It worked both for Ben's birth and for Charlotte's. As beginnings go, they were perfect.

I tried to think of how to restore my son's sense that his parents formed a seamless mesh of warmth and protection around him. But my attempts to map out a route to this goal kept losing their momentum, sucked back into the wallow of "this shouldn't be happening." I so wanted to be done dealing with Allan, and I wanted Ben to be done with him; I knew neither would happen. In desperation, I could almost picture myself leaving the scene—but I could no more walk away from Ben than I could walk away from part of myself.

I consulted with an older friend, a source of good advice who had been through divorce-with-kids herself.

"You should tell Ben," she said indignantly. "You should tell him exactly why you and Allan aren't together anymore. You should tell him how his father betrayed you and broke up your home. He needs to know who's right and who's wrong!"

No, he didn't. I wasn't going to pull Ben deeper into the antagonism, even farther from the sunny bubble in which I'd hoped he'd spend his childhood. I was clear on what not to do, even though I still didn't know how to keep his father from forcing a rift between me and my son.

A few days after that moment in the parking lot, I took both children to the beach. I brought a huge bucket filled with bright plastic molds, and we spread towels and filled those molds with damp sand until we were surrounded by little blobs in almost-recognizable shapes. Then Charlotte napped in her infant carrier, a towel shading her from the sun, as Ben busied himself with digging a hole and I stared at the horizon, watching the waves once more.

One wave can't change a shoreline. Each wave can be so small as to seem insignificant. But if they keep coming, they can add sand to rocky beaches or strip it away, reshaping huge swathes of land in thousands, millions of imperceptible moves over a few years. And no man can stop the ocean.

I couldn't win an open or covert contest with my children's father. I didn't have to force my son to make choices. Instead, I could be that ocean for my son, once again. Instead of trying to persuade, rationalize, and tell my side of the story, I could just send another wave of warmth, affection, and acceptance rolling toward Ben—again and again, throughout the years that stretched ahead. I couldn't say whether, how, or when it would make a difference. All I knew was that this endless, formless plan was the only way I would ever get my son back. Only these waves could carry him to my arms.

I reached over to Ben and rested my hand on his sun-warmed T-shirt, feeling the way his shoulder blades moved as he dug, the motion of the vertebrae in his perfect spine. He turned and looked a question at me. I smiled, looking into his eyes, brown like his dad's. "Love you, babe," I said, and he smiled back.

—Anne-Christine Strugnell

My Second First Date
with My Spouse

I know the exact moment when my marriage ended—that instant when the window of my heart finally slammed irrevocably shut and no amount of kisses or conversation could pry it back open.

After ten tempestuous years, Bill and I finally separated, but months of therapy had failed to move either of us from the stall position to a firm decision. Emotionally, I was stuck in a kind of game show reality where a Bob Barker type was urging me to pick a door. "Well, Karen, door number one is divorce, and behind it lies a world of uncertainty and opportunity. Then there's door number two—reconciliation. Through this door lies security but a possible lifetime of misery. Well, which will it be? The clock is ticking."

This was my weekly contemplation as I sat on the saggy, brown-tweed couch in the worn, sage-colored lobby of our couples' therapist's office. Waiting to go in for our session, my mind would make an absolutely convincing argument one way, then seconds later, caught by the gut-gripping panic of "I don't want to make the wrong decision and ruin the rest of my life," it would go 180 degrees in the opposite direction.

In order to break this cycle of indecision, our therapist suggested that we start dating—each other. In hindsight, I believe that dating your own soon-to-be ex-husband is a very stupid idea. However, at the time, I was desperate and willing to try anything, so at that Wednesday's therapy session we made plans for a Saturday night dinner date—7:00 P.M. sharp.

By the time Saturday rolled around, I had hit the red mark on the anxiety thermometer. Dating etiquette questions danced in my head. *How does one dress for a date with an estranged husband? What would a good conversation-starter be? What if he tries to kiss me goodnight?* Emily Post's *Etiquette* does not cover these circumstances.

So I sat on my living room couch in my flouncy floral dress, watched the clock, and waited. When Bill did not arrive or call by 7:00, I told myself he was just a little late. At 7:15, I was convinced he was on his way over. When the clock hit 7:30, I picked up the phone and called him. There was no answer. Over the next eight hours, I phoned at least ten times, leaving the same message: "Bill, we had a date tonight. Where are you? Are you okay? Call me and let me know what is going on." He never picked up the phone. Finally, at 3:30 A.M., in a state of sheer exhaustion, my head hit the pillow. I had been stood up by my own husband.

I awoke Sunday morning in a groggy state, sheets twisted around my body from an all-night fidget fest. As soon as my feet touched the ground, my hand reached for the phone. Still no answer. I needed to get out of that house.

There is a good reason why the phrase "retail therapy" has caught on. As any woman in the middle of a bad breakup will tell you, in addition to calling your girlfriends to cry your heart out at 4:00 in the morning, shopping is a healing experience. It is often assumed that the soul-soothing qualities of retail therapy lie in the acquisition of new things. I believe that the purchases made during these self-help outings are not the point; rather, it is the cocoon-like environment of the stores that brings comfort.

Walking through Nordstrom early that Sunday morning, the soft lights and live classical piano music playing in the background began to work their magic. I did a pleasant double-take as I passed one of those tilted mirrors designed to add a few inches to your height and remove several from around your middle. I sat at the in-store café, undisturbed, my only companions a hot cappuccino and warm croissant.

Whatever kooky kismet possessed me to do what I did next I will never know. Against all logic, common sense, and self-preservation, I decided to give Bill a call. I was confident he would pick up the phone, provide a plausible explanation, and profusely apologize. I walked with purpose up to the counter and asked the chic saleswoman if I could use the in-store phone to make a local call.

"Certainly," she replied. "Let me dial the number for you."

The phone rang twice before he answered.

"Hi, Bill," I said calmly. "Where were you last night?"

"Oh, um, I, I was right here. I was, um, wondering why you didn't call."

Why I didn't call? "Bill," I said (much less calmly), "I called at least ten times."

"Well, um, I guess I didn't hear the phone ring."

Once, years before I was married and after a bad breakup with a boyfriend, a therapist friend of mine told me, "All the information about a person is available on the first two dates. The trick is that you have to pay attention." She was right. Standing there, my mind retraced the past ten years to our first date, and even then—had I been paying attention, which I clearly wasn't—I could have seen that his need to avoid conflict at all costs and my inherent impatience were going to be a combustible combination.

Now, I am not a lawyer, but I have watched enough popular courtroom dramas on television to know that what happened next constitutes an iron-clad case of temporary insanity. I simply snapped. Years of well-managed anger and denial came pouring out. I unleashed a torrent of R-rated language in a pitch so high and hysterical that dogs a mile away ran for cover, never mind my fellow, well-heeled Sunday shoppers. It is safe to say that nobody has ever cleared a room faster. With a final insult revolving around various body parts, I slammed down the phone.

Mortified, I barely managed to croak out "I am sooo sorry" to the saleswoman, staring wide-eyed at me from across the counter. With a perfectly manicured (and ring-less) left hand, she reached out, patted my hand, and in a tone of true sisterhood said, "Don't worry about it, honey. We have all been there."

That night, no sheets had their shelf-life shortened from my constant tugging, twisting, and turning. The next day I filed for divorce.

—*Karen Leland*

The name of the author's former husband has been changed in this story to protect his privacy.

Like a Horse and Carriage

It took months for my sister, sisters-in-law, and me to plan my parents' fiftieth wedding anniversary. There were invitations to make, a memory book to assemble, and a video of half a century of photographs to be produced. We secretly wrote and recorded a song especially for them. We marked down a hundred RSVPs and ordered the place cards, band, flowers, and blown-up black-and-white photos of their wedding, which would be placed in the center of each specially decorated table.

In their fifty-year-old wedding pictures, my mother and father have that glow before anything happens, as if you could run for miles without ever looking down at your feet, just positive they could never stumble in a million years. In one of the photos, my mother smiles up at my dad like Ginger Rogers at Fred Astaire.

At the end of the party, my folks danced to "As Time Goes By." My mother wore a carefully chosen coffee-colored lace dress, and my father, to my mother's familiar irritation, sported a comfortable old sweater. As the guests began to leave, while the caterers wrapped up the elegant leftovers and the grandchildren gathered up the balloons to take home, I thought about my folks.

Over the years, my parents gave me everything but the one thing they could not. With their fifty years of work and children, grandchildren, anniversaries, Thanksgivings, and camping trips, they just could not show me how to be divorced.

In their selfish pursuit of stability and commitment, they never broke our hearts, never moved across the country, 3,000 miles away from one another. They never sent support payments or formal e-mails arranging visitation. The poor souls had full-time custody of all four of us, all of the time. They couldn't offer me an example of how to date while having three children, how to have a boyfriend once I was thirty years out of high school. My mother was never a working single mother. My dad was always there to handle the bills and the yard and the fixing of broken things.

Obviously, they had no clue.

I'm not saying that all marriages should be saved. Mine should not have been. Still, as angry and as heartbroken as I have been about the demise of my marriage, my heart knows that the bad parts don't erase the good ones. Sometimes the bad parts just make it impossible to stay.

Over the years, the picture of my ex-marriage has come to me gradually, in fits and starts, like a composite sketch of an elusive police suspect. I had to really concentrate on the standout details in order to identify what it was and what it was not. And I had to hold the loss and pain at bay in order to peer honestly back in time to when the marriage was still intact, whole and real.

With some help from my loving, oblivious folks and with some 20/20 hindsight of my own, I think I might have figured some of it out.

Marriage is loads of raggedy photo albums sitting on a shelf in your living room that you just take for granted. It is DVDs and popcorn, robes and slippers, and bad-hair days. It is checkbooks and irritation and passion and taxes and getting to sleep in, or not. It is laundry and taking turns. It is a rather strange breakfast in bed on Mother's Day and a package of snakey worms and smoke bombs on the Fourth of July for the kids. Marriage is not being able to keep your mouth shut about your in-laws, even though you shouldn't have said anything this time or the last time. It is eating drive-thru in the hubby's new car, even though you promised you wouldn't. It's the 2:00 A.M. terrors shared in the dark and doing the Chicken Dance in boxer shorts to celebrate the promotion that will change your lives. Your shared lives. It is knowing each other's history, each other's small stories. Stories you don't have to tell again and again over lattes to blind dates.

Marriage is eating Hamburger Helper by candlelight, because that's what the kids are eating. It is the remote control and gritted teeth and Home Depot and shrunken clothes in the laundry and who gets in the shower first. It's no make-up and sweats and that disgusting, old, torn T-shirt that will not die. It is kids throwing up, or you throwing up, in the middle of the night and changing PJs and sheets and comforting a crying child, and still having to wake up and be functional the next day. It's coffee and the morning paper. It is knowing you will see the person you just had a horrible argument with later that night and the night after that, too. Marriage is no holds barred, no cut to commercial, no time-outs.

Marriage is not dating. Dating says maybe. Marriage says yes. It can be yes for fifty years, and it can fly in the face of every reason to say no.

I have learned all of this now. I just haven't learned divorce. I have no past history of it, no way to glean wisdom from experience, to predict what will happen.

Had my parents been a little more concerned about helping me to understand my future and gotten a miserable divorce themselves—instead of applying their hearts and souls to the process of figuring out how to make ends meet with four kids, arranging summer vacations, and deciding which one of them was going to discipline us—they would not have left me with the indelible possibility of, and longing for, a lifetime of commitment.

They did what they could. And what most of us couldn't.

I always thought it was dopey when a TV audience would clap for a couple who had been married for decades. Big deal, right? But things change. Now, I would probably give them a standing ovation for decades of devotion; for decades of arguments survived; for decades of past, present, and future; for decades of the daily decision to stay.

—Jolie Kanat

Isn't That Special

I named my little girl Therese, after the nurse who helped me deliver her. Therese Castillo stepped right in and became my birthing partner that night—the evening I threw my then-husband, Gabe, out of the soft-blue birthing room and told him never to come back. I suspect nurses are practiced in those kinds of things.

Gabe didn't just leave our marriage like a typical cheating husband, head hung in shame, checkbook hidden. No. Gabe took leave shamelessly, boldly, and with brazen abandon. He could have delivered his practiced speech any time that week, while I did the laundry or readied the nursery. But he waited the way the hawks in the field out by the old quarry wait for their opportunity to swoop down and grab something furry for dinner.

Gabe rewrote our lives on a cold Monday night as angry sleet and freezing rain made roads to the hospital slick and treacherous. While I panted, he planned, waiting and hoping that the evening would deliver him reprieve, forgetting the larger truth ... the arrival of our second child.

As the contractions got closer and closer, Gabe became more and more nervous. Taking a deep breath and gesturing with shaky hands, he said, "I need some coffee."

Coffee? Now?

A forgotten slipper skittered across the floor under his shoe as he lunged from the room.

How odd, I thought, as I stretched for ice chips just out of reach. He had assisted in the delivery of Robert, our firstborn, so why the sudden bout of nerves?

A few minutes later, Gabe stepped back into the antiseptic-smelling room, hands fisted around a steaming Styrofoam cup. He snapped shut his cell phone, just as I was being swept away on the down-draft of another contraction. I looked to him for support, but he looked away before he spoke.

"Look, Carol Ann, I've been seeing someone. And she's really special. And we want to be together . . ."

My mind clicked, snapped, and reeled, like a camera with a broken shutter that keeps clicking but captures nothing at all. My eyes followed a small crack on the ceiling, and my mind took off in flight. *How many years would it take that crack to widen into a bleeding, open fissure of drywall and lathe? Would someone fix the split before it got too wide for repair? Where had my marriage cracked? At what point had I failed?*

". . . because she makes me feel special . . ."

My God! What had he just said? I could only stare at him in my confusion.

Gabe shrugged and began breaking apart his now-empty cup. Then he continued, finding courage in my shocked silence, using that practical tone he usually saved for his clients at tax time. Cheryl, he said, really liked the idea of living someplace with a pool, and his study had taken so much effort to arrange to his specifications, did I think it would be possible for me to move maybe sometime in the next few weeks?

I fought the urge to propel myself toward him until I realized I could hardly move.

As I chewed on ice chips and tried to understand what my husband was saying, I thought I might be sick. I willed myself to push down the nausea, until—splat!—I threw up next to his Italian loafers. I immediately felt better, but then a pall of sadness settled over me like a stifling, too-hot blanket, making it difficult for me to breathe or even form words. Therese didn't even blink; she just grabbed some clean towels and more ice chips. I did notice a tiny smirk around her mouth. I'm sure she had heard the conversation, and from her face I could tell she didn't think much of my husband. Neither did I.

"So, anyway, Cheryl would appreciate it if you would consider leaving the house. She really likes the pool." Gabe leaned down and looked intently at me, willing me to say yes, to let him go.

The pool. A contraction grabbed me like the hand of God and shook me inside out. *His girlfriend wants the pool.* Blood pulsed in my ears. *His girlfriend wants the pool.* "Maybe we could dig it up and give it to her," I croaked, my voice going sideways.

Therese stared openly. I couldn't find the energy to hide my embarrassment over the man who had helped me conceive this child. A trickle of urine escaped as my legs lolled open; tears poured down my flushed face. My eyes burned. My brain hurt. Everything bled together behind my closed eyes, where shapes lost definition. Gabe looked scared, the misery on his face palpable.

Then, slowly, clarity began to emerge from the fog muffling my thoughts. Suddenly, I remembered. The information rose up like a mist. So strange, to be remembering, right then, all those small signs. As I had grown bigger and more tired during my last trimester, Gabe had gotten sloppy, like forgetting a mysterious spa charge on the credit card or insisting on traveling to a last-minute convention in Chicago, a city he had always claimed to despise. When I pressed for details, Gabe had deflected the conversation, rubbing my tummy, kissing the top of my head, making the soft coos he used for getting Robert to sleep.

In a strange way, choosing my labor to take leave of the marriage, although cowardly, provided its own kind of solace. Being so conscious of Therese's birth kept me from doing what I might have chosen otherwise. As another contraction gripped me low and hard, I fantasized: bobbing next to the darting koi and sluggish turtles in the pond at Solitude Park would be Gabe's computer hard drive, a piece of metal holding millions of dollars' worth of information, gently swaying in time with the reeds . . .

I couldn't finish my fantasy—I was about to deliver. And keeping with the spirit, Gabe delivered his final cowardly blow.

"I just need you to know that I have papers, the divorce papers, at home," he said haltingly. "You'll need to sign them."

In his wide, scared eyes I saw our son, Robert, for the tiniest flicker of a moment. Robert, who cried when the little fruit bat living under the garage eaves couldn't fly away and hibernate last fall. My tender

Robert, who collected broken robin's eggshells from the back patio. I choked on a sob. *What would I say to my son? To his new sister I was about to deliver?*

I screamed then, right into Gabe's face, from labor, from pain, from anger—but mostly for my fatherless children. *What a bastard.* Before I could catch my breath, the night-shift obstetrician bustled in, snapping on gloves, acting businesslike.

"How're we doing?" he sang in a friendly voice.

I imagined his wife with an impassioned fury. I watched her in my mind's eye pick out swatches for new dining room chairs or set the perfect holiday table. No matter that I had not seen this gentle man's hands and couldn't possibly know if he sported a wedding band or not. Any woman in his life was not me, was not here, did not feel this vitriolic grief. I tried to control myself, not wanting to pass on the anger and sadness to my baby. Guilt prickled my skin. *Don't make her share this pain,* I cautioned myself.

The doctor smiled at Gabe. "We're doing great!" he sang, as Gabe slinked over to the window, staying well out of the throw of lights near the bed, glancing back at us surreptitiously.

My breathing turned choppy, and my back knotted up with that familiar ache. My thighs burned, and I felt a terrific thirst. *Where was my doctor?*

Where was the ice? I looked around frantically. Gabe continued his absurd sentry of the parking lot out the window, gripping his cell phone tightly. *Where had my husband gone?*

Finally, the smallest gesture—the flick of his wrist on his cell phone to check for messages—enraged me. I felt hot, aflame. I gasped for help, gagged on my own spit, cried for my mother for the first time in twenty years. I would raise this baby alone. Suddenly, a hand fell on mine and began gently stroking my fingers. I will always remember that touch.

"Breathe with me." I looked up to see Therese looking calmly into my face as she demonstrated slow, steady, exaggerated breathing. I knew how to do this. I had done this before. I would do this again. The last time, my husband had been next to me, but not now. Not this time. Not any longer.

"Get. Him. Out."

The doctor looked up, confused, as though I were talking about him.

Therese motioned to Gabe with her head. "You. She wants you out."

Gabe hesitated for a second, looking scared, but then shuffled toward the bed. He looked down at me with a blank face, shrugging. I screamed again, this time right into his blue eyes, wide with surprise. I screamed at him to get the hell out, and I didn't

stop screaming until Therese leaned into me, shush-
ing me. I cried all over the front of her scrubs and
continued to cry right up until my daughter's birth,
about an hour later.

Gabe married Cheryl later that year in a quiet
ceremony, and they moved into their own huge
Georgian home with an even bigger pool. Therese,
Robert, and I moved into a nice townhouse near the
grade school. We didn't have a pool, but we had each
other.

Over the next few years Gabe and Cheryl had
children and built a life. A small town breeds conversation like a light draws moths, so, had I chosen,
I could have learned about Cheryl's new implants or
Gabe's collision with a deer out on Route 28 from any
number of checkers at Muller's grocery. Although I
resisted these conversations for my own sanity, I still
overheard the rumors, as neighbors picked over fresh
produce or compared meat prices. I saw them occasionally, looking happy and seemingly unaffected by
the hidden fissures that had marred my life with
Gabe so dramatically.

And then . . .

The small article took up only about two inches
of space, but it stood out among news of a resigning
county commissioner and a local back-to-school sale.

I pushed Robert's math book aside to read the full story. Cheryl's lawyer had created a public drama around the divorce, rallying support for this mother of two. "No mother with children should be expected to give up her home, after all," he was quoted as saying. As I read the rest of the article, I laughed right out loud.

Gabe had relented, giving Cheryl the house along with alimony and child support. Cheryl modestly claimed not to know what to do with such a big home. But, she explained, she really liked the pool.

—*Sylvia M. DeSantis*

The names in this story have been changed to respect the privacy of those involved.

Roadside Assistance

I love the Windsor police. When they call me this year for a donation, I'll say, "Count me in. I owe you guys one." The Windsor police force is responsible for reminding me to laugh. And, by doing their job, they taught me that, although karma may not be instant, it does exist.

I live only three miles from my ex-husband, and unfortunately, we still work together. This means that occasionally we cross paths on our commutes to and from our now separate homes. I like to avoid these roadway encounters, as they are just another reminder of a life rudely disrupted and of a family reorganized.

One of these dreaded but rare auto encounters occurred late one fall evening. I pulled out of the parking lot at work, and there he was in front of me, stopped at a light. He looked in the rear view mirror and waved—weakly. I gave him an unenthusiastic chin chuck. We entered the flow of commuters with me behind his Jetta, trying unsuccessfully to ignore the irritating way he tailgated the Honda in front of him. It was when we neared Windsor Center that karma first aligned herself in my favor.

We sat in a long line of cars waiting for a light to turn green. When it did, by the time my ex neared the intersection, the light switched to yellow. At that moment, I noticed a police car pull in behind me; my ex did not make this same observation. Just as he pulled into the intersection, the light turned red and he hit the gas.

I stopped at the light, knowing full well that I was about to witness a moment designed to lift my lagging spirits. The officer hit his rollers, swerved out in front of me, and raced off to pull over the eager driver in the little VW. A smile spread across my face, filling me with warmth, and then burst forth in a full-bodied chuckle. By the time the light turned green again, I had composed myself for the drive-by—that delicious moment when I saw my ex pleading with the officer to let him go. I could almost hear him: It wasn't his fault; he was in a rush to get home and feed the fish; why didn't anyone understand him? From the look of the officer's rigid stance, I suspected that his pleas would be ignored and a ticket issued.

Eventually, my laughter mellowed into an incredulous headshake and a satisfied grin. Then my cell phone tone interrupted my reverie. Guess who was calling. It turns out the ex's registration had long ago expired and the Windsor police force was going to confiscate his car and leave him by the side of the road. Could I come and pick him up? Unfortunately, I had not yet learned to say no to these kinds of requests. I should have told him to call his current girlfriend, who happens to work with us. Instead, I drove back, rescued him, and dropped him off at my old house, where the kids were just arriving home from their afternoon practices. It was their night with Dad. They looked surprised to see me and flooded their father with questions. I got a few hugs as well as a few questions that I carefully deflected.

The drive home stood in stark contrast to the drive I'd taken just twenty minutes before. The joy of seeing my ex-husband answering to Johnny Law felt miles away. Karma suddenly seemed less benign and left me with lots of unanswered questions. *Why did I bail him out? Was I going to be forever trapped in helping him fix his messes? Had I moved three miles away to be his mom instead of his wife?*

Well into the night, while I tossed in bed, the answer came to me: I still needed him for roadside assistance too. If my car broke down, who could I call? Most of my friends are married and lead busy lives. I have no family close at hand. Desperation descended, and with it, a solution. I remembered that one of my recently divorced friends, Molly, would pour hot oil over her head before asking her ex for anything.

The next morning I called Molly. It turns out she was trying to break the same old pattern of ex-husband dependence. We now have a pact to be the go-to gal for each other—the person who, without question and without agenda, is there for breakdowns of either our cars or our emotions. We then enlisted one of our married friends, who gladly agreed to be our back-up go-to gal in a crisis.

The morning after setting up my new roadside-assistance team—resolved to be more independent and to be a mother only to my children and not to my ex-husband—the phone rang. I answered, think-ing it was Molly calling back to refine the rescue plan. Instead, it was the ex. He needed help getting the kids to school that morning. They had missed the bus, and with his car in the police compound, he couldn't get both of them to school and himself to work on time.

All my old instincts raced forward, demanding that I fix the messy situation. My desire to see my children as often as possible, especially on days when they are scheduled to be at their Dad's house, further complicated the situation. If I helped him out, I'd be late for work, but I would get to catch up with the kids and send them off to school. As I was about to fly into fix-it mode, Ms. Karma tapped my shoulder. *What about last night?* Although this situation did not demand a call to roadside assistance, it did have all the markings of him creating a mess and my old habit of being his clean-up gal. Had Karma really taught me anything at all? My ex interrupted my deliberations with an impatient reminder that he did not want to be late to work. Neither did I, so I told him he'd have to fix this one on his own.

Thanks to the Windsor police, I remembered how good it feels to laugh. More important, witnessing my ex's traffic violation set in motion a series of events that allowed me to break free of two old habits that had held me trapped in the purgatory known as "recently divorced." While I have other bad habits to discover and break, for the moment I can enjoy a measure of newfound freedom. I can be a good mom who does not turn to her ex for roadside assistance and who has relinquished her role as the fixer. I now also take comfort in knowing that little acts of justice do occasionally get meted out to the deserving.

—Darcy Purinton

The Stepfather Question

Richard and I separated when our son, Ethan, was three and a half. Becoming a single mom wasn't that difficult a transition for me. Richard was not a very involved father in those early years. He worked long hours and started graduate school when Ethan was two. At home, he often sat at the computer well past Ethan's bedtime. Parenthood was my territory as far as Richard was concerned.

This was hardest for me when Ethan was a newborn. I have cerebral palsy; though my case is mild, I lack fine motor skills on my right side and my balance is compromised. This made physically caring for a baby difficult at times. I tried to talk to Richard about it, but he believed I was exaggerating my struggles.

Fortunately, by the time we split up, I found mothering Ethan much easier. I no longer had to figure out how to get things done while holding a baby, and since I wasn't nursing any more, I had full-time access to both my hands again.

Richard's attitude toward fathering also changed with the divorce. Now that he saw Ethan only on weekends, he really focused on his son when they were together. Our breakup was the best thing to happen to their relationship.

It was a good change for me, too. I parented Ethan on my own, as usual, but now I didn't have a husband coming home to tell me everything he would have done differently. For a time, it felt fine that the only men in my life were my father and brother.

When I finally found myself craving male company, I visited my friend Sean from graduate school. We went for a walk in the woods behind Sean's house and laid pennies on the railroad tracks to be flattened. Sean entertained Ethan with goofy voices and elaborate stories. I came home that afternoon feeling ever so slightly in love with him.

"He's great with Ethan," I gushed to my girl-friend Susan. "Interested and attentive. The complete opposite of Richard."

"Okay." She sounded unimpressed. "But how attentive was he to you?"

"Oh, he …" I paused. The answer was, not very.

"Just think about it," Susan cautioned. "Would you want to be with a man who was more focused on your child than on you?"

"No," I admitted. "I'd feel neglected after a while."

"You deserve more than that," she said.

What I deserved. It seemed a radical concept. I'd settled for so little in my marriage. When it ended, I expected to feel bereft. Instead, I found myself exploring great questions: Did I want a man in my life? If so, what shape did I wish that relationship to take? And just how involved should this person be with Ethan?

I didn't know the answers yet. I did know that, after what had become a mostly celibate marriage, I wanted a physical connection with someone.

"I'll find a sex boyfriend," I told Susan. "When that blows over, I'll figure out what I really hope for."

"At least your goals are attainable," she quipped.

I was introduced to Paul at a friend's art opening and made love with him the very next night. He was easygoing, sweet, complimentary—a perfect antidote to the damage Richard had done to my ego.

In the morning, he put his hands on my face and gently pushed at my cheeks with his fingers.

"What are you doing?" I asked, laughing.

"I'm trying to make you un-beautiful. But it's not working."

We started seeing each other regularly. At first, I spent time with Paul only when Ethan was at Richard's or late at night while he slept. Though neither of us planned it, we grew closer. Our relationship soon became a big part of my life. Yet, while Paul was warm to Ethan, he made it clear that he had no desire to take on a parenting role. He was a divorcé with three grown children.

For the most part, Paul's hands-off approach with my son suited me. I liked their playful, bantering relationship. Paul joked with Ethan. They watched adventure movies together. Paul also got Ethan started on playing drums. But if the two of them were awake before me on a weekend morning, Paul would make himself breakfast without offering anything to Ethan. That lack of involvement felt extreme to me.

Dan and I met in a poetry workshop. Blind since birth, he was led into the room and guided to the seat beside me. As the group critiqued one another's poems, I was struck by Dan's thoughtful comments. His writing was well-crafted and moving. I couldn't help noticing that we both mentioned ex-spouses in our poems. Afterward, Dan asked me to walk him to the elevator. He took my arm, and we talked easily as we strolled.

Because I was still with Paul, Dan and I tried to remain mere friends at first. We shared the richest conversations either of us had ever experienced. We talked about books, writing, disability, and relationships. Though he'd been married, Dan never had children. Still, he always asked about my life with Ethan. If I'd had a rough day as a mother or an especially good one, he wanted to know about it. It became clear that our "friendship" was in trouble when we found ourselves imagining having a child together, going so far as to name her. Paul and I broke up a few months later.

I introduced Dan to Ethan on an early spring day in Manhattan. Ethan was shy at first. Having never known a blind person, he studied Dan cautiously. Once, I caught him closing his eyes and feeling his way down a few feet of sidewalk. We went to Union Square Park, where Ethan ran around the playground while Dan read to me from *Poetry Magazine*. After a while, Ethan appeared at Dan's side and brushed his fingers over the Braille.

"Will you take me to the slide?" Dan asked him.

Ethan looked surprised, but he put his hand in Dan's and led him away. I watched as Ethan showed Dan where the ladder was. Laughing and talking, they went down the slide several times. Afterward, Ethan ran toward me. Then, remembering that Dan can't see, he rushed back to get him.

"That was fun," Ethan said before chugging some water and wandering to the jungle gym.

"Seemed like he needed some company," Dan said.

That was two years ago. Now, Dan and I are discussing what it would be like if we lived together. Dan is giving a lot of thought to what his role with Ethan should be. He knows he can't take his father's place, nor does he wish to. Yet, he wouldn't want to just be a roommate either.

"He's important to me," he says. "If I'm going to do it, I want to do it right."

"If anyone can find that balance, you can."

We don't have all the answers yet, but I love how we think about these things together. Meanwhile, I do know the answers to the questions I asked myself after my marriage ended—about the kind of relationship I hoped for. I'm fortunate in that I figured out what I wanted by finding it. Dan is not only sweet with Ethan, he's thoughtful about him. But Dan is also interested in who I am: the poet, the disabled woman, the lover, and Ethan's mother.

—Ona Gritz

This story was first published in the online journal Literary Mama, *March 2007.*

Burned

If you were to watch a made-for-TV movie of my life, it might seem to you that I learn life's lessons more slowly than most. And you'd be right. The most pivotal such lesson took hold only after a crisis that left me standing in my kitchen, threatened by a big, angry man with a pot of boiling coffee aimed at my face.

I got out of the car in an unfamiliar part of town, a shabby area, empty of humanity. A gust of wind pushed on me, as if warning me to get back inside, but—carrying three-year-old Maggie and holding five-year-old Joey by the hand—I headed for the door of the bar, energized by righteousness. I intended to walk into that bar and remind my husband of his apparently forgotten promise to watch the children while I went to a meeting at the preschool.

For months Carl had been talking about this place, but I'd never urged him to take me along to see it. Perhaps I was afraid of what I'd find there. I liked being protected from things disagreeable. Looking back now, I know the children were my necessary shields.

I expected to find Carl inside enjoying himself, talking with his friends, perhaps singing along to the folk ballads on the jukebox, moving from table to table, looking like a San Diego beach bum, a thirty-eight-year-old fake surfer. With no regrets for spoiling his fun, I stepped inside with the children.

At first, it was too dark to see anything, but I could hear recorded music—a woman singing, "Killing Me Softly." This was not a place for laughing surfers and folk-music fans. When my eyes began to adjust and couples on the dance floor emerged out of the blackness, they looked like ghosts meant to scare us. But they were not apparitions; they were gay men holding each other closely. The children tensed. We outlanders didn't belong in this territory. I wanted to get away, but the children were clinging to me, holding me in place.

Dim outlines of men sitting at the counter, heads together, materialized through the smoke from their cigarettes. No one acknowledged us foreigners—a tall mommy with a little girl in her arms and a small boy at her side, refugees just off the boat. Why hadn't I known? I knew Carl liked the company of young men. I knew he stared at handsome male beauty. I knew he chose not to talk about where he spent most of his evenings. I knew he brought home men to stay with us from time to time. But I'd made no conclusions from all that. I didn't want conclusions.

Carl sat slumped at the bar with his back to us, his large bulk dominating the room. The colorful, cheerful blooms of his Hawaiian shirt made him look like some overweight tourist to the islands. Seeing him galvanized my fury at his failing to come home when he'd promised and at his deceptions about this bar. Mostly, though, I hated myself for being stupid, a child mother holding her toy children. Why I didn't dash from the scene amazes me now.

Maggie stared at everything; Joey's hand turned sweaty in mine. Shelves of glasses sparkled with crystal friendliness, and the array of bottles reflected in a mirror behind the bar looked welcoming as we approached. A smiling, curly-headed man in a tanktop, the bartender, stepped back, watching me. The musical refrain crooned over us, and I could smell a sweet, orange-scented deodorant.

Addressing Carl's flowered back, I spoke loudly enough to clash with the music: "Did you forget your promise to baby-sit tonight?"

My husband turned around, stared, and his smile turned fake. The plugs of new hair he's had surgically implanted across his forehead made him look like an aspiring movie extra hoping to be a star. He stabbed out his cigarette, grabbed Joey, and walked out of the smoky room into the twilight. I followed and watched him hurriedly approach his car—a chocolate-colored convertible parked at the curb—place Joey inside, and drive away. For all I knew, they were off to Honolulu.

Maggie and I followed in the station-wagon. Once home, I proceeded carefully up the outside stairs of a house built for people who observe the world from high above everyone else. The edifice rested on a perch overlooking the Pacific like a watchful seabird. Inside, the sound of Julie Andrews singing an offensive contrast to my life at the moment came from the television in the family room, where Joey sat alone, watching *The Sound of Music* on the television.

As I walked toward the kitchen, the sight of a furious Carl standing at the sink unnaturally still stopped me in my tracks. I hesitated in the doorway, surprised and frightened by his glowering eyes. He'd stolen my anger, taken the rage for himself. Every detail of the kitchen pulsated: the painted dancers on my Austrian wall plates, the copper trivet on the counter, the carrot mural on the face of the cupboards. The room seemed a frenzied gallery of malice.

Carl reached for the electric coffee pot on the side counter, jerked it from the outlet, and raised it above his head, watching me like an animal trapped inside a cage. He was going to throw the pot of boiling coffee at me, but I couldn't move.

Suddenly, the lid from the carafe crashed to the floor in a sound like the breaking of the world. It was too late to stop anything, and the steaming brown liquid poured down Carl's gaily colored back in a shocking accident. Every drop fell in slow motion, a lengthening languid stream. It was as though the hot coffee had erupted out of my heart and poured onto Carl's skin, scalding him in a hideous punishment for my humiliation. He cried out, looking at me as if I'd struck him. I stared back, relieved—it was not me.

Carl dropped to one knee, heaving for air like a man about to start a race. The overhead lighting glared and the aroma of coffee filled the air as I watched him take hold of the counter and slowly lift himself to his feet, moaning.

Maggie and Joey appeared beside me. I touched their heads. "Daddy's hurt himself. It's okay. I need to clean up here. You stay out of the kitchen for now." Neither child asked anything or protested. They returned to Julie Andrews and the Austrian hills.

Carl never saw a doctor for his burns, but they healed and he tried to act as if nothing had happened. I had no idea what to say to him. He let me know he didn't want to leave the marriage. He didn't want to live as a single gay man. He wanted to hide behind us, shielded from his mother, from righteous religious folk he'd known all his life, from society. So I didn't take the action you'd want your heroine to take; I didn't initiate a divorce and make my way as a brave single mother. Instead, I waited for somebody to step up and fix things: "Here's what you do. Here's what you say."

My anguish, however, led me to a therapist, where I talked about Carl and me and family and God—all of it. I read books about women who didn't hide behind their children. I read about women who run with wolves, women who love too much, women called "co-dependent." Much of it surprised me. Picture the perfect wife from a sitcom stepping out of the television screen into your living room, taking off her pretty apron, and taking a good look around for the first time. Maybe she puts on shiny new eyeglasses. "Oh," she says. "You mean I could proceed on my own? Make my way?" And you nod yes, and she starts to cry.

Long past the time when Carl's scars were no longer visible, after the therapy and the books, we finally divorced. I took the children and left the aerie on the coast for a home in flat territory, where I could see anything coming from a long way off. Carl moved to a hotel penthouse, where he relaxed into a pleasant coastal life and seemed less afraid than he'd ever been. His mother blamed me for the divorce and refused to notice his change of lifestyle, so he was spared any troublesome parental condemnations.

You may not be surprised to learn that I was happy in the new little house, as free as if I'd been trapped in a cathode tube for thirty years and had been released into full-color, hi-tech, wide-screen reality.

—*Elaine Greensmith Jordan*

This story was first published under the title "Hot Coffee" in the 2007 issue of Fresh Ink, *the annual magazine of Inland Empire Writers.*

Lullaby and Goodbye

I knew it would not be easy; nothing ever is. But there was a moment, a single moment, when fear overwhelmed me. *What was I about to do to my children, to my own life? How could I walk away from the man with whom I shared three sons? Would it be better to stick it out and make sure our boys had two parents?*

While Dave and I sat on the couch talking about splitting our belongings, the words were on the tip of my tongue: "Let's think this over. Maybe there's another way." But I couldn't say them. Something held me back.

"You can have the furniture. I can't take it with me," I said.

"What about the piano? I can send it to you."

"It's not practical. Sell it and send me the money."

He didn't put up a fight. After all, he hadn't wanted the piano in the first place. He couldn't play it, and I wouldn't be there much longer. The piano was really mine, and I could use the money to pay for the divorce.

It was all so cut and dried, so easy to divide up seven years' worth of furnishings and mementos—and to leave behind seven years' worth of travel and holidays, birthdays and anniversaries, love and companionship. The reason why suddenly didn't seem so important. I had to think of the boys. None of us was happy, and no matter what we did, things were getting increasingly more unstable.

Eddie's screams startled us both.

Dave looked up. "I thought I told those boys to go to sleep."

I raced to the boys' bedroom. Eddie sat up in bed, his eyes closed and his head thrown back, screaming. I sat down and pulled him into my arms. "It's all right, honey. It was just a nightmare. Momma's here." He snuffled and calmed in my arms, sobs wracking his body. His shoulders shook. I pulled him onto my lap, his head against my chest, and rocked him slowly as I hummed.

"I heard shouting," he choked through his tears.

It was the same dream over and over: a larger-than-life replay of the arguments between his father and me. Dave and I fought often in the middle of the night, whenever he finally came home, our voices hushed, intent only on ripping each other apart. I thought we had been quiet this time, but Eddie was a light sleeper. He must have heard.

"It's all right, sweetie. No one's shouting. It was all a dream," I reassured Eddie now as I tucked him into bed. Then, I lay down next to him and began singing "Over the Rainbow," the boys' favorite lullaby. He curled up against my side and sang some of the words before he fell back to sleep.

David Scott stirred in the upper bunk. "It's all right, Eddie. It's all right."

I slipped carefully out of the bed and checked on David Scott. He patted the pillow, murmuring in his sleep. "*Shhh*, Eddie. It's all right." I kissed his cheek and tucked the covers around him. I don't know how the boys did it, talking in their sleep to each other as though they were awake. It must be some family quirk, because, according to my mother, my sisters and I carried on entire conversations in our sleep. David Scott stopped patting the pillow and was silent, his breathing even and deep.

No, I couldn't back out now. My boys needed to be able to sleep without nightmares and terrors. I had to go.

Over the last two years, Dave and I had gone to three marriage counselors. We did everything they told us to do, but we couldn't recapture the spark that had brought us together, and Dave didn't seem to want to stop seeing other women. He didn't want to change, and I couldn't change enough. I could no longer ignore the truth. Counseling hadn't worked. Talking hadn't worked. Shouting certainly didn't work. And lullabies didn't soothe whatever it was that made my husband unsettled and uneasy. There was no way to sing my marriage better. The only choice was to leave and take the boys with me. We'd all be better off.

I picked the covers up off the floor and covered A.J. He slept through just about everything, but he was still young. It was only a matter of time before the tension between his father and me would begin to disturb his sleep, too. It was time for us to leave. I looked sadly but resignedly at my three young sons, then closed the door quietly behind me.

A few months later, I sat on the edge of the bed that Eddie, David Scott, and A.J. now shared, singing "Over the Rainbow" to ease them into sleep. The bed was unfamiliar, but they wouldn't have to sleep there for long. We would move out of my parents' house and into our own apartment at the end of the month. Thank goodness, they were still small enough to fit in one bed together.

Together, my sister Tracy and I folded the laundry and talked over old times while the night wore on. Finally, finished with all the chores, I climbed the stairs and checked on the boys before turning in myself. A dim ray of light fell across their sleeping faces. A.J. kicked at the covers and turned over, one pudgy little hand dangling over the edge. Eddie mumbled something about rainbows and wishes, a smile tugging at his lips. David Scott patted Eddie's shoulder, murmuring a trickle of words—"… over the rainbow."

At times I regret the divorce … but not in the middle of the night. There are no more nightmares of fighting and angry voices, no more crying and screams in the night. Now, the only sounds that drift through the night are my boys talking, and sometimes even giggling, in their sleep about little boy things and rainbow wishes. That's when I know that, no matter how hard it is being a single parent, it is all worth it.

I still sing my sons to sleep every night, after the hard days of school and play. But I no longer sing to chase away their nightmares and calm their fears. Instead, I sing a wistful lullaby about hope and better times, grateful we've finally found them.

—J. M. Cornwell

Dating Redux and
Other Cosmic Jokes

"Do you date? Or is that a stupid question?" a former college friend asks when I run into him downtown.

I peer up at Andrew. His hair is still a crest of curls and his cheeks are as warmly dimpled as when we were eighteen. Two decades have passed, yet I glimpse the same shy young man who fell for me our freshman year of college. I didn't return his romantic interest then, back when the landscape of time and expectation spread before me like a welcoming quilt, when I seemingly had my pick of admirers.

Now, on the cusp of forty, I am also on the brink of divorce. The landscape has long since shifted. I am "back in circulation," and re-encounters with former love partners are like popping open the lid on a container of emotions long since stored away.

This isn't the first time I've bumped into Andrew in this university town I call home; the last time we met, I was on the way to my lawyer's office. Now, he asks if my divorce is final. Not yet, I tell him. I have switched to mediation—less messy, less costly, more empowering. He and I chat like old confidantes. His tenth wedding anniversary is coming up. He gives me a rundown on his three small boys. I mention my two children. We reminisce about old roommates.

But the question, "Do you date?" stirs a new beat. Standing in the midday sun, I realize that to the long-married, never-divorced, I am a curiosity.

Once, I was the one with the steady dates and stuffed social calendar, the one who married first; now, by virtue of fate or circumstance or both, I am single again, and Andrew is the settled one worried about finding a baby sitter so he and his wife can celebrate their anniversary.

I tell him about the men I've dated.

"I don't envy you," he says, empathy etched on his face. Or maybe it's pity. I have seen that look before and grew to hate it; now I simply tolerate it.

"It's strange," I say. "But it's fun, too."

Then I launch into the "bennies" of being single again, the dividends of divorce. I talk about enjoying having time to myself while my children are with their father, dispelling the myth that all single mothers are burdened victims and all single fathers absent from their kids' lives. I tell him about camping, hiking, and doing other things I never did while married. I laugh about there being life after separation. Here I am, walking, living proof of it . . . right?

I am aware of trying to sound convincing, jovial even. But after we part, as I ride the elevator back up to my office, I am unable to shake my confusion.

Midlife dating is the ultimate paradox. Early on, I endured the classic rebound relationship—good for the ego but bad for the soul. Then came a string of ineligible men, from the economist to the sandpaper engineer, some divorced or separated, others confirmed bachelors. Getting to know these others at an age when you are all too aware of your psychic blemishes is like going to the ball in rags.

The past week, for instance, has been a tough one, waiting for a call that hasn't come from someone I find attractive and sexy and mysterious. Though I have arrived at a place in my life where I recognize my best points and have made peace with my imperfections, suddenly I feel like fifteen again, focused on the pimple on my chin.

An old friend, a veteran of dating in "middlescence," urges me to slow down, to buck up, to keep my perspective. This advice is not exactly encouraging, given her perspective that, when it comes to dating, the journey is much better than the destination.

"It's like being on a railroad car," she says. "We always want to speed up the ride, but when we get to where we were going, it's never what we thought it would be. The trick is to pace the journey; all that stuff we tend to rush through are the best parts."

If dating again is strange enough, doing it while raising young children only accentuates that strangeness. Once, I met a man who was a writer and liked to dance—two things we had in common. Then we discovered his children were with him on the opposite weekends that mine were with me. After one quick, unsatisfying lunch, we decided to quit while we were behind.

On another occasion, I was talking to an interesting man at an art show when my toddler demanded attention. It was a pickup, but not the kind I'd envisioned. While I held my squirming son closely, I tried to affect an air of nonchalance with this stranger. Moments later, the stench of a soiled diaper permeated the gallery, and mumbling an apology, I rushed to the nearest exit. Suddenly, any possibility of romance seemed remote compared to the urgencies and smells of childhood.

Men who have no children or who have never been married may have more time to get together but be less understanding of the demands on a single mother's time. A friend with a two-year-old went out on her first date in years. They had a good time, and the man started calling her every night just as she was putting her son to bed. When she told him she couldn't talk, he got angry. Eventually, she stopped answering the phone.

Another friend says dating the first time around was bad enough, but that in middle age, the whole thing is a "cosmic joke."

"It's going back to something you never in a million years thought you'd be doing again," she says.

The cosmic thumps can be depressing. There are the magazine articles about how to spot losers. The personal ads from men who are fifty looking for women twenty-five to thirty-five with multiple tattoos, strategic body piercings, and spikey hair. The people who want to fix you up (the implication being that you are broken and in need of repair). The single women friends who inevitably drop out of the loop when they meet a man—adolescence revisited.

But some of the cosmic thumps are intriguing. Dating at midlife is like a laboratory of learning about myself and about the opposite gender. I am experimenting, questioning, discovering. I am reinventing myself. I am finding out what I want in a man (intellect, humor, old-fashioned courtesies), what I can't tolerate (smugness, self-absorption), what I will overlook (paltry hair, cauldron belly, goofy wardrobe). I have trashed the Cinderella tapes that promise happily ever after. I am not looking for marriage or a life partner. There are many things worse than being single and dating at forty: going home to a man who criticizes or ignores you is one; being lonely in a marriage is another. Dating again comes with a certain amount of risk and drama, of living for the moment, that is wonderfully freeing. The cosmic joke continues, but now I am laughing.

The attractive, sexy mystery man may or may not call again. In the meantime, I go for coffee with a musician who has been married three times, who is older than me by a decade and shorter by a head, who exudes a Zen-like fascination with dating.

"Every person whose path crosses mine enriches me," he says. "As soon as you start thinking about what comes next, you miss out on the moment."

When I run into Andrew again, I will update him on my divorce and the men in my life. Will I remain a curiosity to my long-married college friend? Maybe. But it doesn't matter as much. I'm giving a wink and a nod to new journeys at mid life.

—Tina Lincer

Smithing My Life

My eyes were level with Mother's fold-down desk, where she sat paying bills. I had to stand on my tiptoes to watch her write a check. First the date, 1945, and then the amount. Finally, she wrote her signature at the bottom.

"Why do you sign your name 'Mrs. Frank Kavanagh?'" I asked. "Why don't you use your own name?"

"It's what girls do, dear, when they get married. Only divorced women sign their own first names."

I could tell from the way she said "divorced women" that she never intended any of the Kavanagh females to become one.

She laid down her fountain pen and smiled. "Someday you, too, will get a grown-up name."

I gathered that, for some reason I could not fathom, married women lost their names. You could have a first name or a husband but not both.

I spent the next fifteen years spelling *k-a-v-a-n-a-g-h* to every clerk and bureaucrat, then having to insist it was Kavanagh with a *k* and no *u*. At college in the fifties, I met a man named Smith and congratulated myself on falling in love with a man with an easy-to-spell name. I looked forward to changing my name to Mrs. Smith. I'd never considered Smith a distinguished name, but when I thought about it, the name represented many skilled trades: blacksmith, silversmith, goldsmith.

At our wedding, a beefy man of about fifty barreled out of the crowd in the parish hall with two women in tow. He shook my hand with a gorilla grip, introduced himself as my father-in-law, and then introduced his daughter, Nancy Smith, and his wife, Elsie Smith. "Some are born Smiths; others have to marry one." He punched Elsie's upper arm.

I rubbed my hand, wondering if he meant I wasn't a real Smith. What difference did it make how I got the name? From that day forward, by gosh or by marriage, I was a Smith.

On our honeymoon, my new groom and I stopped at a romantic hideaway on the Oregon Coast. My husband registered us, of course, as Mr. and Mrs. Smith. The motel clerk's raised eyebrow let me know he thought we'd made up the name just to get into his motel. I thrust my left hand toward the clerk to flash my shiny new gold wedding band. We were legal Smiths.

During the sixties, the man named Smith left me for a woman named Jane. After our divorce, they married, but Jane did not become a Smith, possibly because the name Jane Smith would have shouted anonymity, like Jane Doe. It helps to have an unusual first name like Sheila when you're a Smith.

By the seventies I had been a Smith as long as I had been a Kavanagh. Even though the relationship with its original owner hadn't worked out, the name Smith represented my initiation into adulthood. Despite my ex-father-in-law's disparagement, I considered myself a genuine Smith.

One day while on a walk with a recently divorced friend, she said, "I'm taking back my birth name. Call me Wilma Munson from now on." Wilma's decision was common during the heady first days of women's liberation, when many women took back their birth names after their divorces.

"But that's your father's name." I said. "It still represents a woman taking some man's name."

"It represents who I used to be before I got married. Are you getting rid of Smith?"

"Only the man, not the name."

Wilma grinned, then turned serious. "I thought you were into women's lib."

"I am. It means I have a choice."

She shook her head. "Odd choice."

"Everyone knows me by Smith. Besides, if I went back to Kavanagh, I'd be spelling again."

"Yes, but . . ."

"And I've grown fond of Smith. The word means someone who crafts goods from raw materials."

"That's the kind of person we can all aspire to be," Wilma agreed.

Then I met a man called Odegard, who was careful with money and claimed to believe in the liberation of women. Just the kind of man I'd been searching for. I moved right in with him.

One evening we'd gone out for dinner to a restaurant where he had a two-for-one coupon deal. After dessert, he pulled a small cardboard box out of his pocket. His blue eyes twinkled. "Can I call you Mrs. Odegard?"

Odegard. It sounded like a deodorant.

"Are you proposing?" I batted my eyelashes.

He opened the box to reveal a zircon ring.

"I'd like to marry you, but I want to keep being a Smith." I laid my hand over his. "Changing my name would make it difficult for my friends to find me."

His eyes narrowed. "You want to use the name of your ex-husband instead of mine?"

"Yes, I do. I get to choose my name. I'm a liberated woman."

"I'm liberated too." He paused. "We're going Dutch."

I stared at him. I intended to stand firm on the name issue.

Finally he said, "I can let you keep that name."

"Good. I just changed my address on all my subscriptions using Smith."

"Wouldn't want to waste postage," he said in all seriousness. He slipped the engagement ring on my finger.

We had our wedding reception in our backyard. Steadying myself on the slick grass in my best flat shoes (no high heels for this liberated woman!), I met the Odegard relatives for the first time. They grilled me about why I planned to remain a Smith. Wouldn't using Ms. Odegard be good enough?

His unmarried sister asked through pursed lips, "Are you a professional?"

Just what kind of professional did she mean? I arranged my face into what I hoped was a chaste smile. "Laboratory technician," I said.

In addition to letting me keep my name, Odegard let me do many things—except I had to ask permission to do them in the first place. Along with allowing me to cook our meals and clean his house, he allowed me to work to support the household. Only one of us chuckled when he introduced me to his friends as his paying housekeeper.

By the time that marriage went sour, no-fault divorce had made dissolving a marriage easier than getting a driver's license. Never having used Odegard in any context, I filled out the legal paperwork using the name Smith. I found a place to live, loaded up my share of our stuff, and changed my address on my subscriptions once again.

On the day my divorce decree was to be granted, I climbed the steep steps of the county courthouse looming against the gray Oregon sky and entered a high-ceilinged courtroom made solemn with dark wood paneling. The American and Oregon flags lurked in the corners.

The judge frowned at me over half glasses. "I'm adding to your decree that you may keep the name Smith."

"Thank you, but I never used the name Odegard."

"Just in case there's a problem down the road."

I couldn't imagine what was going through his head. Could Jane steal my name? Could Smith decide I couldn't retain it? What did the judge know about the Odegards that I didn't?

He thumped his gavel. The State of Oregon had pronounced me a permanent Smith.

In the eighties, I fell for a man called Schmidt. When he proposed marriage, I said yes, but I wanted to keep my name. He said he wanted me to use his.

"Schmidt means Smith in German," he persisted.

I shook my head no. "I like Smith better."

Finally he offered a compromise: "We could hyphenate our last names."

I doubted Smith-anything would have the ring of just plain Smith, but I tried his suggestion on for size, "Smith-Schmidt, Smith-Schmidt, Smith-Schmidt . . ." "Too many adjacent consonants," I joked.

All of a sudden his face grew red and the artery in his neck pulsed. "You think you're too good to be Schmidt!" he shouted.

I broke off the relationship.

I smith my own life.

—*Sheila Smith*

Something in Common

"You have to think outside the box," the impeccably dressed instructor admonished us.

"If you're not outside your comfort zone, you'll stay right where you are," the polished businesswoman persisted.

Too late for me, Jill thought. A forty-nine-year-old recent divorcée with an unimpressive work history and total financial devastation, Jill sat in the midst of a group of women with whom she had nothing in common. This "career transition" program was a last resort, the end of the line.

The internal dialogue kicked in. *I've submitted dozens of resumes; why haven't I found a job? The present living situation can't last. But how can I change it? Sitting in a classroom won't produce stability. If it were not impolite to walk out, I'd go . . . where?*

Jill dragged her focus back to the speaker, a confident professional with a no-nonsense but personable approach to the business of rescuing women who had fallen or been cast into the abyss of emotional or financial distress. Even her first name, Elizabeth, exuded both authority and serenity.

"This is not an old-fashioned 'touchy-feely' group in which everyone whines about life's unfairness. Nor is it a place where we prepare a resume from a template and send you on your way," Elizabeth said, glancing from person to person. "My job is to help you garner all your resources, skills, and desires, so that you can get from where you are to where you want to be . . . one step at a time. This doesn't happen overnight, ladies."

Jill grudgingly admitted that the speaker's style—commanding, yet calm— was easy to listen to, comforting almost.

"What if you've only taken care of the house and kids for twenty years?" This question came from the somewhat disheveled woman sitting across from Jill.

"Did you ever pay bills, manage a budget, organize a neighborhood watch, or volunteer at school?" Elizabeth replied.

The woman began taking notes. So did Jill.

"In this program, we will not be looking backward, nor will we dwell on the present. We'll look forward only," Elizabeth went on. "During the next five weeks, we'll examine not only skills, but also likes, desires, and motives. Many of you are desperate to find a job. But ignoring the intangibles—the social, emotional, and spiritual aspects of life—can stifle your job search. Look around, you may discover you have much more in common with each other than you thought possible."

Jill's face flushed, and she didn't dare look directly at Elizabeth.

"In fact," Elizabeth continued, "we're going to break the ice and begin to get acquainted by playing a fabulous game called 'vacation.'"

Jill hated nothing more than the shower-type games.

"As we go around the room," Elizabeth explained, "each person will say her own name and will name an object, beginning with her name's first letter, that she plans to take with her on vacation. Then she'll restate the names and vacation objects of all who have gone before."

Protests echoed around the room but were ignored as the rest of the career-transition staff entered the room to join the festivities.

As the game proceeded around the room, Jill concentrated with all her might on the names and vacation objects of the other women in the group. She could think of nothing else and Jill started to panic: *What am I going to bring? Think! What will I bring?—I know!*

"My name is Jill. I'm taking my private jet on vacation, and everyone's invited!"

Laughter and cheers erupted.

"Desiree, diamond; Anne, apple; Connie, cat; Lisa, lion..." Jill continued matching names with objects, and when she got to the last person, she realized she was smiling. When the game was over, Jill looked around and discovered she knew everyone's name.

Visibly relaxed, everyone, including Jill, gave Elizabeth their full attention as the seasoned veteran of rescues expounded on the virtues of balance and of focusing on all aspects of life.

"A proactive approach toward health is essential. Tomorrow morning, we'll have nurses and speakers from Regional Hospital here. For those who are interested, they'll do blood draws for conditions like diabetes, high cholesterol, and thyroid disease. Afterward, we'll have breakfast and then you'll hear from speakers on topics such as nutrition, stress management, and where to get free mammograms and other tests. Come prepared for a good time, because we'll have several door prizes."

This announcement was met with enthusiasm and apparently unlocked inhibitions, as conversations sprang up across the room. Without insurance for several years, Jill had been ignoring these medical procedures. An almost unrecognizable sense of positive anticipation began to permeate her consciousness.

"Do you live in the city?" the soft-spoken woman on Jill's right, Anne (apple), asked.

"No, I live about fifteen minutes outside the city."

"That's what I thought," Anne replied with a shy smile.

Somewhat taken aback, Jill said, "What about you?"

"I live downtown, about ten blocks from here. Connie and I walked over together; it takes about fifteen minutes."

Before Jill could reply, Elizabeth's voice could be heard over the hubbub. "A couple of announcements, ladies. During this first week, we'll have a drawing each day, a little incentive to keep you coming back. Look under your chairs, please. Whoever has number twelve will take home this lovely, black cherry candle."

To Jill's shock and delight, she had number twelve. Black cherry was her favorite candle scent.

"Okay, moving on," Elizabeth said. "I have an assignment which is due day after tomorrow. You need to bring a detailed list of every task, duty, and responsibility you've ever had, whether at work, at home, or as a volunteer. This list is important. Write the assignment in your planners. Now, for those who need bus passes, I have them here."

As Jill envisioned having to ride the bus, she turned to the woman on her right, Lisa (lion). "Do you have an extra pen? Mine just ran out of ink."

"Sure. I always have plenty. My brother has a stash of company pens in a jar by the front door."

"Oh." Jill wasn't sure how to respond.

"I'm staying with my brother and his family, which is pretty horrible, but I don't have a choice right now," Lisa said matter-of-factly.

"I understand." Jill replied. "I'm staying at the home of my parents, who are in their seventies."

"I have my own bedroom there, but my brother's wife wants nothing to do with me, so I stay away from the house as much as possible."

"Well, I could have a room upstairs, but I prefer the basement apartment." Jill felt a release valve open as she finally shared this information without embarrassment. "It's completely finished, and I have a kitchen and an office. I can't believe there's someone else who has to live with relatives."

"I think we're doing okay. I heard Anne and Connie talking about going back to the shelter."

Momentarily speechless, Jill looked outside and noticed it was raining.

Lisa continued, "My husband left ten years ago, and I've been taking care of my mother ever since. When she died two months ago, I'd been out of the workforce all that time, had no job and nowhere to go. My brother said I could move in, not knowing his wife would be such a witch."

"I'm sorry about your mother," Jill said, "My parents are in good health and are pretty independent. I don't pay rent, but I help out—cleaning house, errands, some cooking. I have my space; it's just the idea of not having my own place."

"I can't even set my purse down, unless it's in my room. Wish I had the basement," Lisa said. "Do you want to meet for lunch some time? It sounds like we have a few things in common."

"Absolutely," Jill said.

Fifteen minutes later, Jill was backing out of the parking lot to head toward the freeway. Still chilled from the rain, she stopped at a red light and shuddered involuntarily, anxious to be in a different part of town. Glancing to the right, she saw two women walking close to the buildings under the overhang: Connie and Anne. Impulsively, Jill opened her window. "Do you two need a ride?"

They ran over and climbed in.

"Are you sure?" Connie asked.

"Do you know your way around here?" Anne wanted to know.

"Just tell me which direction to go," Jill said.

"Straight ahead, ten blocks," Connie pointed. "I'm glad you came along."

"I am, too. Thanks," Anne said. "You said you live outside the city?"

"Yes. Actually, I'm staying with my parents for now."

"You're lucky." Connie said. "I lost my job three months ago, and I don't have a family. A master's degree in municipal government is getting me nowhere."

"You have a master's degree and can't get a job?" Jill said incredulously. "I have a bachelor's in interior design, but for years, I've only done freelance off and on. I'm afraid I'll wind up in retail or clerical."

"My cousin owns a business that decorates offices. I think it's on Broadway. I'll write down the name," Anne said. "All I have is high school; I'd take any job to get my kids back and get some order in my life. Here we are. Pull over here."

"Tomorrow will be a good day," Connie assured Anne and Jill as she opened the car door. "I know someone who went through this course, and she said the health day was fun."

Instead of taking the freeway, Jill decided to drive back through the city. She noticed that each neighborhood blended into the next yet managed to retain its own personality, with clusters of unique small businesses and the occasional franchise elbowed in. She turned north on Broadway and stopped at the Espresso Boutique. She made her way to the counter through college students, businessmen, and retirees.

"I'd like a decaf cappuccino. Do you happen to know where..." she paused to look at the name Anne had written, "Expressive Concepts is located?"

"Right here." The college kid behind the counter looked up and pointed to the ceiling.

Jill took the stairs to the second floor. A preoccupied man sat at an ornate antique desk amidst rather unappealing furniture arrangements.

"Excuse me," Jill said, "I was referred by a friend, Anne Crawford. She said you may have a job opening."

The man stood up and looked at her for a long moment. "Any experience?"

"I have a bachelor of arts in interior design, and I've worked in department stores and also done freelance decorating for several businesses."

He began searching through chaotic piles of paper on his desk and finally handed her an application. "Obviously, I need help here. Can you complete this and drop off a resume with a couple of references next week?"

"Yes."

As Jill pulled into her parents' driveway, she imagined getting off a bus and running through the rain toward a women's shelter. "Hi, Mom," she called as she entered the front door. "I picked up a roasted chicken; thought I'd fix a salad, too."

"Thanks, dear, but we're going out for supper with friends. By the way, you had a call from an Elizabeth somebody. She wanted to remind you to fast tonight after midnight for a blood draw tomorrow morning."

When her parents left, Jill descended to what now seemed like a castle. She brewed a cup of toasted almond coffee in her kitchen, went to her office, lit a nutmeg candle, savoring the rich aroma and the pleasure she'd felt when giving Anne the black cherry candle. Then she turned on her computer, and far from either a box or a comfort zone, she began the list of her capabilities and strengths.

—Jocelyn Duval

The names of the people in this story have been changed to protect their privacy.

Under the Big Top

A three-ring circus, starring:

Megan, my daughter, class of 1996
Shannon, my stepdaughter, class of 1996
Ex-husband #1, Megan's dad
Ex-husband #2, Shannon's dad
Ex-husband #1's new wife and stepson
Ex-husband #2's ex-wife, Shannon's mom
Ex-husband #1's parents, Megan's grandparents
Ex-husband #2's new girlfriend
Shannon's brothers and assorted others
And me as the tightrope walker

In June 1996, my daughter Megan graduated from high school, as did my stepdaughter Shannon, who had been living with me since Shannon's father and I had separated the year before. So the girls and

I decided it would be nice to have an open house to celebrate the occasion. We should just have called it Barnum and Bailey and let 'er rip.

Shannon wanted to invite her mother from Tennessee. W-e-e-l-l, alrighty then. I reluctantly agreed. It was Shannon's graduation, after all. She'd worked hard for it. But, since she was traveling so far, her mother couldn't very well come for just the afternoon; she had to come for the whole weekend, and her funds were limited, so she had to stay at our house. She and I had always gotten along, from a distance, anyway. So I said okay.

But Shannon's mother didn't want to drive alone from Tennessee to Pennsylvania. So she brought Shannon's two teenage brothers (who, let me add, have had brushes with the law) as well as Shannon's Tennessee boyfriend, who, two weeks earlier, had left his condoms behind when he'd come for Shannon's prom.

Send in the clowns.

For the entire two days she was here before the event, Shannon's mother obsessed about my house, changing pictures around on my walls, taking down our Halloween spiders (okay, I know it wasn't Halloween anymore, but we really liked them), and incessantly cleaning. The night before the open house, she stayed up till 3:00 A.M. scrubbing my living room baseboards. I tried a couple of times to discourage her, but then gave in. The baseboards probably needed it. What the heck? My nerves were shot anyway.

Shannon's father still lives here in town. To tell the truth, he was okay. He'd cooked up several large bowls of food and came over early to help set up tables in the yard. His new girlfriend was another story. She dislikes Shannon's mother greatly. Greatly. Stay tuned for that act.

Then there was Megan's father and his wife and his parents. He hadn't been speaking to me ever since I started pushing for child support. So I expected his usual surly attitude. Except, by the time he and his wife arrived, his parents—with his wife's son in the car—hadn't gotten here yet, and she just knew, protesting hysterically, that they were lost or dead in a ditch or . . . Needless to say, this diffused him considerably. It was one of the first occasions I'd had to be grateful for his parents' unfortunate behavior.

All the players finally arrived, whole and healthy, and the graduation went by almost without a hitch. Fortunately, we managed to avert the majority of a shoving and shouting match that erupted between Shannon's father's girlfriend and Shannon's mother on the bleacher steps of the high school gymnasium. At least they waited until after the ceremony. Most of us kept walking toward the door, pretending we didn't know any of those screaming people. After all, the girls had friends they wanted to kiss and hug as we left the school, their eyes lit with pride, all the graduates in their black gowns and hats another reminder of how they were all growing up and would soon leave our nests.

Although cloudy skies had been threatening to break open all afternoon, the rain held off, for which I will be eternally thankful. Although it is a good-sized house, the potential firepower of all those people locked inside together would have beaten any of nature's pyrotechnics outdoors.

Over the prior several days, I had managed to coordinate food donations for the party from family and friends, and everyone ate, drank, and at least appeared merry. As people came, I played the master of ceremonies and made sure everyone knew every one else, mediated squabbles with the siblings, and directed people to the food. As always, my sister coordinated a watermelon fight, as that is one of her primary family roles, but no one hit the grandparents, testifying to our amazing juggling skills.

Megan shared her time diplomatically between the bride's side and the groom's side of her parents' attendees, all the while wearing a huge, striped Dr. Seuss hat. The requisite photos were taken against the green background of our fresh-mown grass—I had to make Shannon's boyfriend useful somehow— and the parents sat back and let the children enjoy their moments of glory.

By 9:00, the dancing ladies and elephants had all gone home, and we had cleaned up the remains. The girls were excitedly comparing graduation presents, and the siblings were, of course, squabbling. Shannon's mother continued to hover, deep-cleaning the counters and restacking the dishes, but my nerves had eased once the party was done. She could have rewired the fuse box, and I wouldn't have cared.

While the precious passing of parchment from administrator to student was the most important moment of the day as history goes, the most memorable for me was later that evening. Shannon chose an opportunity while her mother was occupied with her sons to pull me aside for a big hug and a bouquet of flowers. "I know it wasn't easy for you this weekend, and you didn't have to do this. I just wanted to thank you," she said.

That still brings a tear to my eye, even now, and made the whole ordeal worthwhile. It isn't easy to put your own resentments and feelings aside, and it certainly isn't easy to make other family members do so as well. But knowing that the children benefit from the effort and that they learn from our examples are the best rewards in the world.

—*Barbara Mountjoy*

A Clean Heart

On what would have been my seventeenth wedding anniversary, I invited a group of friends to bless the house that my ex-husband, Roberto, and I had once owned together. A judge had signed our settlement agreement, making our divorce final, several months earlier. In between bouts of rage, I'd grieved the end of our marriage, ritualizing its death by burying my wedding band and an anniversary photo in a pot of soil. With a prayer for transformation, I'd also planted a cutting of pathos vine in the pot and placed it in my room. As friends now stepped into my house, I felt grateful that they were gathering to christen my new life as a divorced woman and a single mom.

Stacy, my pastor, blessed my threshold with salt, reminding us of tears but also of salt's curative power. My other friends followed with poems and prayer flags, each one blessing a separate room in my house.

In my bedroom, the last room to be blessed, we ringed the bed I'd shared for so many years with Roberto. Holding hands with my friends, I stared at my new quilt; the squares of white roses interspersed with patches of green leaves blurred through my tears. My friend Jan spoke eloquently of transformation and invoked our prayers. When it came my turn, I nodded toward my potted vine and the small photo I'd placed among its leaves. The picture showed me heading out for my writing class, a parka slung over my shoulder and a grin flashing across my face. I prayed that I would be the mother my daughters needed: the new Lana, the one smiling in the picture, setting out to write. Lowering my head, I gave into my tears and let my friends hold me in the circle of their linked hands.

For my daughters' sakes, I knew I had to pull myself together, to hang on to my full-time grant-writing job, and to steer myself through the wreckage of divorce. But I felt unsure and apprehensive in my new life. As I'd requested, the girls lived with me. Roberto visited them on Saturdays, but we spoke little, and I refused to ask him for assistance in household repairs or other areas of his expertise. I wanted to prove that I could stand on my own, but the truth was I felt cut off, vulnerable, and alone. The risks seemed greater. The unknowns seemed to multiply.

Could I make the mortgage payments? Could I keep up the repairs on an old house and an old car?

I hadn't always been this way. In my mid-twenties, I'd stared down men armed with automatic rifles in my efforts to accompany refugees in war-torn El Salvador. I'd driven across the Arizona desert in a car that didn't always start and died once mid-trip. But during seventeen years of marriage, I'd grown accustomed to my spouse fixing things that went wrong. When he betrayed me, it shook me to the core. How could I have loved and trusted him so much that I'd blinded myself to his deceit? Could I ever trust my own heart again?

I wanted to believe in new possibilities for my life, but I felt wounded and bitter. My friends urged me to consider a spiritual retreat, so I signed up for a few days in a monastery that a co-worker recommended. As the date approached, I made arrangements for my daughters, but I began to feel anxious about being away from them and our familiar routine for four days. The retreat center was located several hours away on a windy coastal highway, much of which I'd not driven before. As I packed, I fretted about my fourteen-year-old car's ability to make the drive. The unknown terrain exacerbated my anxiety.

At 3:00 A.M. on the eve of my trip, I lay awake in bed, unable to sleep, my heart pounding in my chest as if I'd just run a marathon. I delayed my trip and went to see a doctor the following day. After looking at my electrocardiogram, she told me my heart was fine. She mentioned the possibility of a panic attack and added that heart palpitations were one of the more aggravating, but completely normal, symptoms of perimenopause. Her reassurances should have relieved my anxiety, but in my newly divorced state, I was fretful about anything I could not control. My ability to trust had been broken, and I feared all things beneath the surface—the plumbing and wiring in my old house, the engine in my old car, and now, the changes in my aging body.

That night I eventually lulled myself to sleep with a novel, and the next morning I braved the long coastal drive to the monastery where the retreat was being held. I was given a small trailer, one of eight "hermitages" tucked like boxes under the hillside's smattering of oak, madrone, and chaparral. From the trailer's deck, I glimpsed a blue pocket of ocean glistening between the trees. A small lizard darted off the trailer steps as I unloaded my bags. Setting them down on the deck, I breathed in the tranquility of the surrounding hillside. My car and I had made it.

The trailer housed a tiny bathroom, a desk, a bed, and a rocking chair. A card on the desk explained the importance of silence, instructed how to obtain meals and bring them back to the trailer, and listed the times of the daily matins and vespers. Imprinted on another card was the order's Brief Rule of Saint Romuald. I lingered on its final phrases:

> *Empty yourself completely and sit waiting, content with the grace of God, like the chick who tastes nothing and eats nothing but what his mother brings him.*

Suddenly overwhelmed with gratitude, my eyes welled with tears. Here, I could be my scared, trembling, solitary self. I could wait in the arms of God and learn to trust again. For the next two days, I meditated in the mornings and wrote in the afternoons. I attended Eucharist and vespers with the monks and with other silent retreatants, but I quickly returned to my hermitage, relishing my solitude and my time alone with God.

On the third morning, I rose and went to sit in the wooden, straight-backed chair beside the desk, my chosen spot for morning meditation. Soon, a chant from the liturgy of my childhood lilted into my mind of its own accord:

> *Create in me a clean heart, Oh God, and renew a right spirit within me.*

In the old Lutheran hymnal, the red one with the corners frayed pink, this portion of Psalm 51 had been sung as the offertory. Now it entered my silence with words of hope:

> *Restore unto me the joy of thy salvation and uphold me with thy free spirit.*

As I continued in my meditation, the words of the chant drifted away and my flesh-and-blood heart, the one that had pounded four nights earlier, moved with an easy rhythm. I breathed deeply, my chest rising and falling, the air rushing in and out, like the sound of the waves below.

In the year since my divorce, I'd grieved and raged. I'd been angry at Roberto for his deceit but also at myself for loving blindly. Yet, in that year, I also had meditated daily. I'd scribbled through numerous journals, seen a therapist, and attended church regularly with my daughters. In that year, Roberto had paid child support like clockwork, picked up the girls consistently on his appointed day, fed them dinner, and dropped them off at my house. Despite the fact that I'd told them of their father's infidelity, our daughters had forged ahead with their classes and friendships. At school and at home, they seemed buoyant and content with their lives. They'd told me time and again that I was a great mom.

Sitting in silence at the monastery, I both acknowledged these facts and allowed them to slip from my mind. Breathing deeply in and out, I turned the corners of my centering prayer. Outside, the brush burst to life with snapping twigs, rustles, and birdsong, and I invoked God's presence as a mother. "Mother," I intoned, waiting like a chick for nourishment. At the root of my being, I felt peace.

Later, as I basked on a bench overlooking the ocean's expanse of sparkling blue, I realized that I no longer hated Roberto, even though his loathsome secrets had once seemed eternally unforgivable. He'd seduced his teenaged niece, and he'd concealed the affair from me and his sister, the girl's mother, for more than a year. His actions had wounded me deeply and had devastated two families. Yet, time and distance had enabled me to somehow accept the reality of his transgression. More important, I realized that my mistaken trust in him did not predestine me to a life of continuing error. Nor did his betrayal undermine my worth. Instead, I saw that I could now choose to remember the love that had once existed between us and move on. I could affirm myself and begin to trust my heart again.

Even so, a clean heart is not a new heart. Upon my return from the retreat, my sometimes amicable behavior toward Roberto did not signify that I had forgotten his bad choices or that I condoned his decision to live as a couple with his niece. But letting go of my bitterness enabled me to focus more fully on the developments in my life. I completed my writing program and volunteered my writing skills to benefit homeless families. I signed a contract for a small book. Outside of work, I arranged for the necessary repairs on my house and car and took time to enjoy my daughters and their successes in school, martial arts, and theater. I signed up for an online dating service and began to meet new people. My confidence grew, and my fears subsided.

Months after the retreat, I opened my bedroom window to let in the breeze and noticed an abundance of leaves on the vine I'd planted with my old wedding band. I thought of the photo buried at the pot's bottom—the picture of Roberto and me holding hands on our thirteenth wedding anniversary—and I remembered a fleeting vision I'd had years earlier. While meditating, I'd glimpsed Roberto and myself buried in the cold ground. Pressed between soil and rocks, our supine bodies had lain suspended without touching, without need or want, and a tree had sprouted from us, its roots extending up alongside our bodies, piercing the topsoil and thickening into a trunk crowned with branches, fluttering leaves, and small red apples. At the time, several years before our divorce, the vision had perplexed me, but now

I saw its message of transformation. In burying the "me" in relationship to my ex-husband, I had grown into a new existence, one that was beginning to bear fruit. I liked my freedom to rise early and meditate, to write at night or read until I fell asleep. I liked talking and traveling with my daughters and the new life we were creating together.

Turning from the vine, I gazed at a large, framed portrait of my six-year-old self that my mother had given me. I'd hung it squarely above my bed, replacing the seascape I'd once found askew over sloppy bed covers, signs I'd overlooked in the days of my blindness. Staring now into my younger, blonder self's smiling, wide-eyed expression, I saw a child who knew she was loved.

Opposite the portrait hung a gilded mirror, and I turned to gaze at my forty-seven-year-old face. With the divorce, more wrinkles had settled about my eyes and mouth, but I no longer viewed my aging body as something to fear or disparage. Instead, I saw a strong woman I could trust. For the first time in many months, I looked into my reflection and I saw love.

—Lana Dalberg

The names of some people in this story have been changed to protect their privacy.

Answering the Dreaded Question:
Are You Dating Anyone?

I don't know how to date any more.

The last time I dated, I wore polyester pants, a quiana blouse, and platform shoes. I was in college in the late 1970s, living near five thousand other people my age—half were single men. My calendar was filled with dances, football games, and mixers. I still remember one record stretch when I had a date with a different boy for seven nights in a row.

Now, I live in a quiet suburban neighborhood with my three children and two dogs. I can think of only one single man within a three-mile radius. My calendar is still filled with football games, but of the pint-sized variety. Occasionally, I chaperone a junior high dance. My only record-breaking accomplishment is winning "yard of the month."

Single for more than seven years after an eighteen-year marriage, I can count my dates on one hand, including the one my mother arranged.

I seem to emit a high-frequency signal detected only by single men: "Alert. Single woman nearby. Run for your life."

When a single man and his daughter moved into the house behind me, I treated him like any new neighbor and casually walked across the alley behind our houses to introduce myself.

I haven't seen him since. If I step out the back door and catch a glimpse of him, he darts into his garage and closes the door. When he pulls into his driveway and sees me outside, he stays in his car.

I was considering telling him that his cold, reclusive ways were unacceptable in our friendly neighborhood when I realized what was going on. Other well-meaning neighbors must have told him about the single woman who lived behind him. The poor man is waiting for me to throw the lasso around his neck.

I'm often asked if I'm dating anyone. The question makes me feel like an eighth-grade wallflower again, trying to figure out how to answer my Uncle Harold's annoying dating questions.

"Do you have a boyfriend?" he'd ask.

"I'm in-between boyfriends right now," I'd reply.

Dating has changed since I was in eighth grade. I've noticed a new pattern when my children date. Girls tell my boys, "You will date me now." The boys follow along until they are given other orders. My daughter seems to have the same power over the boys she dates. One of her boyfriends once followed her command to come over and watch *Sound of Music*. My sons came to me, concerned that Zach really wanted to watch a movie featuring Julie Andrews. Soon after, I spotted one of my sons watching *The Little Mermaid* with his new girlfriend.

I'm not sure I am interested in this highly controlled dating, but it seems to be the trend.

I know women who have tried speed dating, enrolled in just-for-lunch dating services, and dated men they met on E-Harmony. One single friend spends every Friday night reading law magazines at the bookstore, hoping to meet a fellow lawyer.

Is dating really worth all this time and effort?

On my ideal Friday night, I settle at the kitchen table with my scrapbooking supplies and watch decorating shows on HGTV.

One evening my teenage daughter breezed past me, leaving an aura of perfume in her wake. She looked at me and shook her head. "Mom, you've got to get out more."

Once a year I allow myself to be persuaded to go on a blind date. It takes a year to get over it before I agree to another. Blind dating has forced me to admit that I have a double standard. I color my hair and wear bracelets, but I'm not interested in men who do.

As my last blind date droned on over dinner, I found myself wishing I was doing something else— watching the Weather Channel, cleaning out my e-mail inbox, organizing my sweaters.

Suddenly it dawned on me, I don't owe Uncle Harold or anyone else an explanation or excuse for not dating. Maybe the reason I send an invisible "don't date me" signal is because I am quite content with my life as it is.

I like to wear jeans and tennis shoes all weekend and go to chick flicks with my friends. If I have a free Saturday afternoon, my favorite pastime is to plant perennials in my garden. And I love serving a big Sunday dinner to a table surrounded by hungry teenagers.

I may decide to enter the dating jungle someday, but for now, my life is full of blessings.

No, Uncle Harold, I still don't have a boyfriend, but thanks for asking, I'm doing just fine.

—Nancy George

Bruised but Not Broken

I'm waiting for the phone to ring. It will. When my husband takes a weekend with buddies, a hoarse whisper interrupts my sleep after the phone's shrill ring. I always hang up immediately and take the phone off the hook, hearing only the caller's first words, "Your husband . . ."

Tonight, I won't hang up. Tonight I want to know. Does the caller plan to tell me of the long absences, too long for just a quick trip to the bank? Of the phone bill with new charges to an area code I don't know? Of the sudden need to buy a present for some coworker's birthday? The cocky sound of his voice when she called our house one weekend?

Midnight. On the dot. I reach for the phone on the first ring.

"Hello?" I make my voice firm, alert, unyielding.

"Your husband . . ." Again, the hoarse, creepy whisper, like an obscene phone caller. Does he hope I'll just hang up?

"Yes, what?" I demand.

"He's screwing a coworker." His voice is flat, uninflected.

"Who are you?" Again, I ask with authority. I'm no longer the shrinking coward I have been.

"He said he was going camping, but he's not. He's in a motel with his coworker. Just like every other time he said he's going fishing, but really went fornicating." Now, he sounds excited, delighted with his own phrasing.

"Thank you."

He hangs up. I replace the phone in its cradle. He may call back. I want to know more.

I've known in my heart, for how long, a year? I want to scoop the kids out of their beds and drive to my mom's. That's what I do when I'm lost, I run to my mother. But instead I go back to bed, tossing and turning, fuming, plotting revenge.

In the morning, I make a run to the grocery store, leaving the kids and puppies propped into the corners of the worn-out denim sofa in front of the television, sleepy bundles on the couch, delighted with this treat. Normally, the kids get to watch TV before breakfast only when they're sick. They aren't sick. I am.

The aisles blur; I can't concentrate. I don't know what I'm buying. Potato chips, mac and cheese, tamales, hot dogs, cookies. My mind repeats other words, words I have known only in books: adulterer, fornicator. He will call home tonight to tell me about his camping trip, his hike in the Sierras, how lonely he is. Bullshit, all of it. He hasn't left the bed of the motel.

Stupid little man. Stupid piss ant coward. I hate him; I loathe him. I will not spend another night with him in my bed. I will not live under the same roof with him. He must leave.

I would leave this minute, fly to Tonga or Brazil, if it weren't for the kids. Our daughter, at ten, is a fire-brand, athletic and rough and silly and charming. Our son is quiet and studious, adoring all of us with worshipful routines to please his sister, his mother, his father. Dear little boy, he keeps each of us on a pedestal—his father's, the highest.

We drowse through the day with a jigsaw puzzle at the kitchen table, fast food for lunch, tamales for dinner. Lassitude hangs in the house like an echo from our innocent past.

"What should we do tomorrow?" I ask them, looking for a distraction. Soon enough, adults will break their hearts.

"The movies!" says Bobby, his new front teeth gigantic in his small mouth. He grabs the newspaper to choose something we'll all like. "*Karate Kid II* is playing on Parthenia."

"The beach!" squeals Kip. Blonde braids flying, she spins toward the garage to look for her boogie board.

"Mmmm," I hedge. "How about both?"

"Yay!" they yell.

"I can't wait until Dad calls so I can tell him," says Bobby. "I miss Dad."

He curls morosely for a moment into the chair. Though he is only seven, Bobby is as sensitive as a young poet. He looks at the world and feels its pain. I cannot allay his fears about meltdowns at nuclear power plants and overpopulation. I simply read with him, listen to him, provide hope for the future.

I can't wait for Dad to call, either. I think of the various poses I will assume with him.

The day winds down. The kids have watched *Foul Play* on video, and we've all read for a bit. The house creaks with quiet. Dad has not called yet. Figures. He's very busy, you know. The kids go to bed without talking to him, though earlier Bobby picked up the phone twice to listen for the dial tone, checking to make sure it worked.

The phone rings late. I know it's either the prodigal husband or the hoarse man. Either way, perhaps there will be answers.

"Hi!" he yells too exuberantly. "Are the kids up?"

"Of course not."

"Shoot. We got back late from up the mountain," he lies, alluding to his fictive camping buddy, Elias, who is really named Coco. I picture the mountain of their flesh together, and my throat convulses in a gagging gulp.

"Yeah." I clench my jaw, wanting to confront him, to shame him. I want to hang up on him; I want to spit into the phone.

"Well, I'm bushed."

I'll bet you are, quite literally, creep.

"I'll be home before dinner tomorrow, unless we get a late start."

The rumpled sheets, the sunlight through the motel's cheap drapes—a late start, indeed.

"What are you and the kids going to do?" he asks with predatory innocence.

"I don't know." I'm not lying. I don't know what I'm going to do. The beach trip tomorrow seems a long way off. I will do something. I have to do something.

As it turns out, I do nothing, for two more years. Well, that's not quite true. I fall into a depression so deep that I often cannot get myself dressed. For Christmas, he buys me a new robe. I know they laughed together when she asked him, "What does she like to do?" and he told her, "Sleep." The two love birds must have had quite a chuckle over that.

I have quit speaking to him. I go to bed when the kids do.

Finally, he sits on the edge of the bed and says to me, "No one goes to bed at eight-thirty."

I look up from my book. "I do, and I'm someone."

I look down again, but speak in a clear, loud voice, eschewing the mumble I've been using for so long. "I know about you and Coco." It just comes out.

He sighs deeply. "How long?" He will not look at me.

"Two years."

"How do you know?"

"I won't tell you."

"What do you want me to do?"

"Sleep in the other room." That's all I can think of.

He does so. We tell the kids it's better for his back, but they know better. Kids know plenty.

Eventually, I see a psychologist. She calls me a survivor. She helps me to develop a game plan. I confront the lying bastard, not with a scene in front of the kids, but with a letter left on the bureau. I can write what I cannot say.

I take the kids to see Grandma, leaving before he comes home from work. The letter is in plain sight, detailing the lies I know about, the phone calls, all the indicators he thought he had hidden so well.

He doesn't call me while I am away.

When I return, I begin to cook dinner. He sneaks up behind me, embraces me, tries to nuzzle my neck.

"Stop it." I jerk away, and he steps back.

"I'm sorry. Too soon? We can see a counselor together."

"Maybe."

We have to try, I think, for the sake of the children. But it doesn't work. Six weeks of face-offs in the neutrality of the counselor's office only make me loathe him more. I intuit that he's been sneaking around for several years, possibly having had affairs with different women even as far back as when I was pregnant with Kip. The sight of him nauseates me.

My psychologist finally convinces me that I must start over.

"But the dogs? How can I find a place to move that allows dogs?" This is my last line of defense against change.

"The dogs are dogs," she says. "Get them new homes and get yourself a life."

Interesting, new, forthright advice. The dogs are just dogs?

We divorce, sell the house, find the dogs good new homes. I move to an apartment; he moves to a condo. We share custody. The kids go through depression and acting out—fury around the house, apathy in their classrooms. Bobby begins pulling his hair out by the roots, and I surface from my self-absorption to embark on a campaign of recognition of my son's goodness, his smart ideas, the joy he brings me. The hair-pulling ends.

It's her junior year, and Kip's grades are a concern. I meet with her counselors and teachers and sit at the table with her to work through chemistry equations. Her grades go up. She earns the right to drive, and I do my best to quit white-knuckling the armrest on the passenger's side, acknowledging her skill and confidence.

Me? I'm happy. I feel free, unfettered, new. I've met a man who lives across the hallway. I locate my *self* again. I'm actually in there, under all these layers of chenille robe, frustration fat, and sorrow. I'm whole in all my parts, stronger after my big break. The kids are, too. We have lived through a nuclear-family melt-down—devastating, but not fatal. We are survivors.

Eileen Clemens Granfors

The names in this story have been changed to respect the privacy of those involved.

New Year's Resolution

It must have been in 1980, because I remember it was on a Wednesday and New Year's Eve Day fell on a Wednesday that year, when a stranger sitting next to me on the train invited me to ride to the end of the line with him. This chance meeting, just as the old year was turning into the new, gave me a glimpse of what would be most important to me in the years to come.

The train was all mixed up. I was going home hours early, and so were many others, and the bustle of our boarding had reached the suburbs of confusion. Commuters honor-bound to the usual confident gait, although on unfamiliar platforms, found different configurations of coaches, seats, and lavatories; some people confirmed they were on the right track by hailing old friends and even nodding to familiar strangers more vigorously than usual on this staid commuter railroad.

Trainmen were on the alert, verifying that we all knew where we were and where we were going. The conductors assisted early celebrants up the high steps with a boost to the elbow and a convivial warning and protected the upholstery by seating selected merrymakers close to the vestibule trash baskets.

Regulars from the evening trains—our usual people in unusual seats, their familiar faces mixed like new cards ready for a poker game—were shuffled with a scattering of strangers on this late afternoon run out of Hoboken. I was out of sorts. Tired, dirty, hungry, and grouchy, I was reading a magazine I usually save for home and resenting the unwanted weight of a gift bottle of champagne relayed to me by my teetotaler boss. While I was traveling, my friend, Pearl, her two young daughters, and my two young sons were decorating my house for our first (and what would be our last) joint New Year's Eve celebration.

Because of last-minute boarding conventions, I was out of place in an aisle seat on the right side of the train; I always travel outbound in a window seat on the left. For a while, my seatmate co-read my magazine over my shoulder. Then he took advantage of our irregular rush hour to break protocol and ask, "What is it you women want, anyway?"

My response was the commuter's cold, nonverbal, noncommittal acknowledgement that said, I heard you, but I don't want to hear you again. Yet, he continued.

"My wife has everything: a car, a swimming pool, a big house, clothes. Everything she could want. What's wrong with that?"

Sounded pretty good to this woman, with a minimum-wage job of uncertain security and two kids to support.

"And do you know what she does? I can't understand it. She gets a part-time job. At the mall. Selling dresses. Dresses! She could have any dress she wants. Any dress."

I never talk to strangers on the train. I'm usually too tired for pleasantries or too protective of that rare, private, mental telephone booth time I use to change from Clark Kent worker to Supermom. But it was a holiday and he was more exasperated than inebriated, so I bit.

"Does she have anything you haven't given her?"

He didn't understand.

"Anything she was able to get for herself? Anything without asking you or that you didn't pay for? Anything without your stamp on it?"

"Why should she? I give her everything she wants; she doesn't even have to ask."

"What did she do all day before?"

"Nothing. Stayed home. Like everyone else."

I nodded. I knew better than to try to explain that the very lack of specifics in his description of her life implied her function and contribution were invisible to him. I returned to the magazine I no longer was reading.

"Why do you work?" he asked.

Why am I riding the train home from a job when I expected to spend my days with my young children, cooking pot roasts and listening for the train whistle's signal my husband would soon be home and it was time to heat the vegetables? Why do I board the 6:23 A.M. train when my younger child has an earache and I'm unsure whether my hurried arrangements to get him to the doctor will work out as planned?

Fortunately, the loudspeaker's familiar song gave me the gift of silence: "Plauderville, Plauderville. Next station stop, Broadway, Fair Lawn. Broadway, Fair Lawn, next station stop." I grabbed the opportunity to begin very early departure preparations.

"You're leaving?" he asked.

"Soon."

"Don't."

I turned away. My resumption of commuter ano-nymity was long overdue, and he had caught my instant withdrawal into suspicion.

"Ride to the end of the line with me. Please." He told me that he would pass his stop, too. That we would get a cab back to his car. That he would drive me home. "Please," he said. "There won't be any trouble."

"I can't," I told him, without the polite smile or regrets one gives another.

"I don't mean anything by it," he added. "I just want to talk. I have to understand. Why is she doing it?"

The train whistle that used to tell me when to put the fire under the vegetables was announcing our approach to my station stop, and I stood up to take possession of my turn in the aisle to grab my coat down from the overhead rack.

"I have to go home. My children are waiting; my friend came over with her kids; we're celebrat-ing together." I was surprised to be giving him an explanation.

He asked again.

"I can't. I have friends and family waiting," I told him once more.

At that moment I heard myself and looked hard at him, and saw that I was on firmer ground than he.

All I didn't have was someone to give me everything I wanted. Everything else was at home.

I left the train at my usual station, leaving the bewildered and beleaguered stranger to journey on alone through the mysteries of marriage.

Despite all our good intentions, New Year's Eve fizzled out.

By the time I got home, I didn't have a stair climb left in me and never saw the kids' basement decorations. We ordered pizza, and while we waited for its delivery, we ate some appetizers the girls had made and uncorked the champagne. The kids were delighted they were allowed to bring the whole pizza box, except for two slices, downstairs with them. They had all the privacy they needed to celebrate the New Year with as much noise as they wanted and drink unlimited soda and polish off the candy, chips, and pretzels without us.

Pearl and I quietly ate our slices and toasted our survival of the old year with one glass each of bubbly. We talked for a while, and my friend announced her ex-husband's impending remarriage. Not long after, Pearl fell asleep on the loveseat soon after we decided that neither of us coveted the groom but both of us envied the honeymoon trip to a tropical isle. I was sprawled on the living room floor when the Sandman visited ahead of Father Time, and I dozed off realizing that I had been too tired to see the romance of it all.

For, on a New Year's Eve when I was feeling sad and beaten, for whatever reason, a stranger invited me to go to the end of the line with him. And he didn't even know I had a bottle of champagne in my purse.

Time validated the insight I developed on that train ride more than twenty-five years ago. Here's an update.

My friend Pearl and I each had some loves in our lives. She became engaged but cancelled the wedding. I spent most of those years working, sleeping, riding the train, and wondering how commuting, divorced, single moms found time to find new partners.

Both our ex-husbands remarried; mine divorced again.

When it was time for college, Pearl's kids left northern New Jersey for Boston and Washington, D.C. One of her greatest fears had been that her daughters would have to go to work to support themselves after high school. Yet, she was able to cobble together grants and loans for them. One girl is an accountant, the other a lawyer.

My greatest fear was that my kids would go to college far from home. They did not. Both continued their educations in northern New Jersey. They often used the same train line, although in different directions, to visit on weekends and to carry leftovers back to school.

More than ten years ago, Pearl bolted for a beach she loved in North Carolina. But she made the distance seem small by setting up her long-distance phone service so we could keep in touch without going bankrupt. She came back north to bring me home from the hospital after major surgery and to drive me to my younger son's funeral.

Until our kids all married, we were able to avoid public occasions where we had to be polite to the men who, in our opinions, did not give their children enough financial or emotional support. Yet, we were our children's supports when each dad successfully battled serious health issues.

To this day, we bemoan lost opportunities. Pearl had been unable to move to another state with her children to further her career. I had been unable to accept jobs that required unplanned travel or weekend and holiday work. She and I forged our way, with our children, at a time when kids could not each lunch in school in our suburb, when potential employers asked about birth control methods, and when television portrayed divorced women as "hot to trot." Now we speak of those times with more nostalgia than anger.

Just last summer, my son and Pearl's older daughter met, along with their children. My son could not get over how much older Pearl's daughter had gotten; she could not get over how tall my son had grown. They had not seen each other since they were teenagers, yet each expected the other to have remained the same.

Pearl and I are each other's memory sticks. I am the only person to whom she can say, "Remember when . . . ," and she is the only person to whom I can say, "He's behaving the way he did when he was seven years old," and we both know what we mean.

I am proud of my wisdom back then, when a stranger invited me to go to the end of the line with him. Despite fatigue and the discouragement of the moment, I knew what would be most important to me in the years to come: my friend, her two kids, and my kids, waiting for me at home.

—*Marilyn A. Gelman*

Honeymoon for Four

As I walked down the aisle on my father's arm, I had mixed feelings: I was glad to be marrying the man I loved, but I was not looking forward to our honeymoon. It's not that I didn't want to go away with my new groom. Quite the contrary, I wanted nothing more than to start our new marriage with a few blessed days alone together. But I had been unable to find anyone I could trust who was willing and able to take care of my two young daughters, eight-year-old Emily and three-year-old Sarah, during the week we'd be gone. Believe me, I had tried. My parents had to work, and my ex-husband was not willing. So my soon-to-be new husband, Steve, and I would just have to go on our honeymoon with the kids. Isn't that what all families do nowadays, the second time around?

The day after the wedding, the four of us traveled to "the cabin," a two-room house my new father-in-law owns on Bull Shoals Lake in Arkansas, seven hours away from our northern Missouri home.

"Are we there yet?" Emily asked the typical question.

"Not too much longer," I said, looking from Emily to Sarah to Steve, my husband of less than twenty-four hours. I wanted everything to be perfect. I wanted this to be our great new start as a real family. It had to be, I reasoned. Wouldn't this honeymoon be an indication of how strong our marriage was?

We drove up and down the Ozark Mountain roads that eventually narrowed. Thick forests lined the highway, which was more like a country lane. Each curve in the road brought new sights, so different from the prairie grasses we were familiar with. The deep color of the evergreen forest contrasted with rock and clay; wildflowers bloomed in the May sun.

We finally arrived at the cabin. The air smelled fresh, with the lake just a few hundred feet away. Relieved we were finally there, I started unpacking the bags of groceries we had brought. Then I looked down at Sarah, who was sitting at the table. Her face was flushed, and she had placed her head on her hands.

"Are you feeling okay, honey?" I asked.

She started scratching some red blotches on her arms. I recognized the symptoms of chickenpox, which Emily had suffered through just a few weeks earlier. We should have known; it was just a matter of time.

With his usual calm logic, Steve explained to me that as long as we kept Sarah comfortable and safe from too much sun exposure, her chickenpox would not slow us down. There was a small motor boat for our use, but we would need to buy life jackets. We piled into the van (with Sarah covered in calamine lotion, her favorite blanket, and wearing a brimmed sun hat) and drove to the closest shopping mall, which was about thirty minutes away.

After making our purchases, we headed back to the cabin. We were on a steep incline when we stopped at a red light behind a semi-tractor-trailer. My husband realized he had stopped too close to give the truck room to roll back when it started up the hill. There was a car close behind us, though, so we couldn't back up. Luckily, there was a road to the right, and Steve decided to turn.

After we turned off the main road, my feelings changed from hope to despair as the hours passed and the cabin was nowhere in sight. I felt increasingly agitated as we drove around those mountain roads trying to find the way back to our cabin. Steve was wasting our precious time, time we could have been spending out on the lake, relaxing and making family memories. How could he believe he would find a way back without a map and without knowing the area? I looked at Steve, the man who I had vowed I would take "for richer or poorer, in sickness or in health," who I would have followed to the ends of the earth. That was yesterday. Today, I wasn't sure I wanted to follow him another minute.

Sarah started sobbing. "I don't feel good, Mommy."

"It won't be long now," I said, without much conviction.

Steve sighed. I looked at him again, and my heart softened. I knew it wasn't his fault. He was trying his best. And there weren't many homes along the way to stop and ask for directions. I was sure Steve wanted to be out on the lake just as much as I did. How foolish I felt to blame him. Silently, I asked for forgiveness. My rush of anger subsided at the same time we saw a log home in the distance.

Thank goodness, Steve stopped, but it was just for a second. There was a sign posted on the big front porch that stated "no trespassing." He drove on.

We saw another home, a small white house with a young woman working in her garden. Steve stopped and talked to her, but soon walked back to the car, shaking his head. The woman had no idea how to get us back to Bull Shoals Lake. We drove on and crossed a water-filled road despite a warning sign. I said a silent prayer of protection.

We stopped a third time, and a woman in a skirt and blouse came outside to talk to my husband. I saw her raise her arm and point in the direction from which we had come. Back across the water, back around the mountain, back to the "no trespassing" sign. Finally, we saw the sign directing us to Bull Shoals Lake.

We arrived back at the cabin, and within a short time, slathered in sun block, we had donned our new life jackets and were cruising in our motor boat. Perhaps we would create our first happy family memory, after all. I chatted excitedly, happy to have the unpleasant events of the morning behind me. The breeze caressed my hair, and the water calmed me. All of a sudden, I realized my feet were wet—something was terribly wrong. I looked down and saw standing water lining the bottom of the boat. It had sprung a leak. We were sinking. Without a word, Steve adjusted the tiller, and the boat sputtered. We barely made it to shore.

Clouds gathered as we made our way to the cabin, and then it rained steadily for the next two days.

We stayed inside the cabin, playing games, reading, and getting to know each other in a new way, as a family. Steve had not been married before and wasn't used to being around children. The first week of his married life was a baptism by fire. He learned what it was like to be up in the middle of the night with a sick child and how children could argue about nothing at all, and we both realized it wasn't going to be easy.

I didn't get my wish to have a perfect honeymoon. Far from it. But now, sixteen years later, we can laugh about it.

Six years ago, we drove to the cabin and reminisced. Over the years, since the 1960s when Steve's family bought the place, each guest has written in a guest book: his name, the date, and a comment about what they did or how they felt. I had forgotten about the book, but upon our arrival at the cabin, I eagerly looked for our names. There they were! Emily wrote in her eight-year-old scrawl, "I like the swings at the playground," and I had written down what Sarah had told me: "I like swimming on the sandy beach." I wrote: "I am in awe of the beauty of the Ozark Mountains. The scenery is breathtaking!" And Steve wrote: "It's good to be back at the cabin. I have so many fun memories of visiting here when I was a kid." There was no mention of our misfortunes.

It was fitting that we went to the cabin again that summer. Our first family outing had been at that cabin, and now, with eighteen-year-old Emily about to go off to college and thirteen-year-old Sarah about to begin her transformation from little girl to young woman, it was a good time for memories. During that second stay, no one was sick, we didn't get lost, and we didn't ride in a leaky boat.

These days, Emily is thinking about getting married, and occasionally we talk about where she might go on her honeymoon. I can think of no better place to begin a marriage than in the little cabin on Bulls Shoals Lake amidst the beautiful Ozark Mountains. Although her honeymoon will not mirror ours, Emily—and I—understand that you don't need a blissful honeymoon to have a wonderful married life. Even though our honeymoon for four was not picture-perfect from beginning to end, neither was it without its joys. Those first family memories we made at the lake cabin proved to be an important block in the solid foundation upon which we built our happily ever after.

—Amy Houts

It's About Love

When Neal and I decided to put our families together almost thirty-five years ago, we had no idea how rewarding and, yes, how challenging the journey would be. As clearly as though it were yesterday, I can hear him saying, "If we're going to make this work, we're going to have to love them all as our very own." And that is exactly what we tried to do. Of course, we had struggles, just like any other family. But over the years, signs of cohesion began to appear, and friendships between the children began to develop. Through thick and thin, we loved them all. It was the only way we knew.

Eventually, the children grew up and married, and later, grandchildren came along. Loving those little ones was a natural extension of the love we shared with their parents. We felt so blessed.

Our last vacation together as a family occurred in St. George, Utah. We decided to rent a three-bedroom condo and invite the kids. "You all come, just don't all come at once," we told them. We didn't get them all there, but we got half of them there, and we loved every minute of it. Just as the friendships between the children continued to grow, so too did the friendships between the grandchildren. What a joy it was to watch.

When Neal died, I promised him that I'd love the children for both of us, and I meant it sincerely. It wasn't until the kids arrived for his funeral that I began to understand the depth of what we'd forged. The children all wanted to stay in our home. That meant we had people sleeping in every room except the kitchen. Some were even on the floor, but they didn't seem to mind. The house became one big dormitory, with sleeping bags in every imaginable place.

It was wonderful having all the children under one roof. And it was interesting to see how they interacted. There were no "his" or "hers." They were all just family. I'd see different assortments sitting out on the deck visiting, other assortments going for a walk and talking. I couldn't help but think how pleased Neal would have been to see the bond between them. We really were a family, after all.

Neal and I had planned to fly to Portland, Oregon, in August of that year to visit our oldest son and daughter and their families. Even though we lost Neal in June, I decided to go anyway. Shortly before I left on my trip, someone asked me how many children I have. Automatically, I answered, "Six."

"Six children! Really?"

"Well, yes."

"And they're all yours?" the woman persisted. It took a while before I realized what she was getting at, and when I did, I actually had to stop and figure it out.

Not long after that, someone else commented about how nice it was that I kept in touch with my stepchildren. "They are my family!" was the only thing I could think of to say, but in my heart the seed of doubt had been planted. *What if I didn't belong in their lives anymore?* I could hardly bear the thought. So that was the first thing I asked when I got to their home in Portland. I just had to know. The thought had never entered their minds.

Fifteen years have gone by since we lost Neal, and we are just as much of a family as ever. Some of the grandchildren are now grown and married, and four great-grandchildren have been added to the assortment. Somehow, the love just grows and grows.

The crowning glory of it all, I think, was when I flew to Portland recently to see my grandson, Chris, graduate from high school and to celebrate his eighteenth birthday. I also wanted to watch him and his sister, Meredith, play baseball. Shortly after I got there, Chris and I spent more than an hour talking. His phone would ring now and then (of course), and each time he would say, "Can I call you back? I'm visiting with my grandma." I can't tell you how honored I felt to hear him say that.

It was a wonderful week. We laughed a lot, played hard, and slept as little as possible. Midway through the week, Chris started telling me about some poems he'd written. Being a poet myself, I was delighted. "Maybe you get that from me, Chris. Do you suppose?" He smiled and answered, "Probably."

Later, when it occurred to me there actually is no blood between us, I felt a bit silly for having said that, and I told his mother. She turned to me and looked me squarely in the eye. "It isn't about blood. It's about love."

—*Donna Miesbach*

This story was first published in Valley Living for the Whole Family.

Just Fine

A yellow U-Haul is parked in the driveway across the street. I stand at my window and watch people carry cardboard boxes, lamps, and armloads of clothes into the truck. I know, only too well, what's happening.

One morning last summer, my neighbor, Pat, and I had coffee on my deck. Shadows from the tree overhead played on Pat's gray hair. She looked every bit of her sixty-two years.

"Don and I are getting a divorce," she said. Just like that. "We've been married forty-three years; the last twenty have been hell." She told me more details than I really needed to know, then looked into her coffee cup and paused. "I found a mobile home not too far from here. I'm moving out at the end of the month."

A memory pinched inside. "I know you're in a lot of pain right now, but you will get through this.

It may take a while, but you'll be fine." I put my hand over hers and hoped I didn't sound too preachy or like some kind of a divorce counselor.

Twenty years ago, my best friend, Katy, who'd also been through a divorce, said something like that to me. I was as doubtful then as I'm sure Pat must have been when her marriage was ending.

Twenty years since my divorce . . . Has as it really been that long?

I couldn't wait to go off to college, to be a writer. Armed with a journalism degree, I'd cover fires and train wrecks and bank robberies. I'd live the reporter's life—a desk in a noisy newsroom, writing against a deadline. Instead, I fell in love, married Jim, and had a family.

My babies grew into teenagers, and Jim scrambled up the corporate ladder, which left him with little time for me and the kids. Feeling like an emotionally abandoned housewife, I took my frustrations out on the tennis court.

One hot July afternoon after a long set, Katy and I cooled off on a bench. "Jim's so involved in his work he doesn't even know I exist." I picked up my water bottle. "We've been growing apart for years, and I can't remember the last time he said he loved me. We've tried counseling; that didn't work. I never thought it would come to this, but I'm thinking about a divorce."

Katy put her arm around my sweaty shoulder. "I know how you feel, but you'll get through this. You're stronger than you think. It may take a while, but you'll be fine." I nodded to be polite, but couldn't imagine how I would ever be "fine."

Tension at home grew worse every day. Jim seemed disinterested in everything, and when he didn't have a business dinner or late meeting, he holed up in his study with the door closed. I wanted him to care about me, or at least to act like he did, but after a while, I stopped caring too. The dark hole that had started to grow in my heart felt like it was getting bigger every day.

A few weeks after my conversation with Katy, I watched Jim in the garden, watering his tomato plants. A smile crossed his face. I walked outside, maybe we could talk.

"What are you smiling about?" I asked.

"That was quite an office party last night."

I had stayed home with a good book. I'd had it with boring office parties, standing around in my politically correct black cocktail dress, making small talk with someone I hardly knew. Jim gently picked one of his tomatoes off the vine.

"Debbie, my new manager, told me I was a great guy and if anything ever happened to my marriage, I should call her."

Why would he tell me that? I'd seen her a few times, blonde and always dressed to the nines. She was smart, attractive   everything I wasn't. Was she the reason he wasn't home much anymore?

That night I lay in bed and listened to Jim snore. He'd been asleep for hours. We still slept in the queen-sized bed we'd bought as newlyweds, but as far away from each other as possible, arms and legs pulled in tight, careful not to touch. Even though we hadn't made love for months, the thought of him in bed with another woman made my stomach lurch.

Conversations between us were either arguments about what was wrong with each other or polite remarks laced with animosity. Thoughts of divorce swirled in my head. I needed space, somewhere peaceful and quiet, with no memories, where I could think. Though a divorce would change my life forever, I realized that the love we once had for each other was gone and wasn't coming back. Staying here in the house we had shared for so long would only make things worse. After months of sleepless nights and tension-filled days, I needed to take what was left of my pride and move away from the shouting matches and cold stares, try to find some peace and quiet—and myself.

The next morning, I called Katy. "Help me find an apartment," I said. We looked at a few apartments, and by the end of the afternoon, I'd found a modest one-bedroom. I wasn't picky. But now I needed to tell Jim.

For the first time in months, Jim's Buick turned into the driveway before seven. We'd lived in this two-story white house for fifteen years. The pillars flanking the front door that I had once thought so charming now seemed more like bars on a cage.

Jim opened the door, set down his briefcase, and went upstairs to take off his suit. I knew the drill. Next, he'd ask me to fix him a drink; a shot and a half of Gilbey's gin, three ice cubes, and Schweppes tonic.

For the last time, I splashed the gin over the ice cubes; the tonic water fizzed to the top of the glass. My heart felt like a wooden spoon banging against my chest. I picked up his drink; the glass cooled my sweaty palm. Jim wasn't a violent man. Words, not fists, were his weapon of choice. Still, I wasn't sure how he'd react.

"I've got something to tell you." I handed him his drink. This wasn't going to be easy.

"What is it now?"

I took a deep breath and tried not to look nervous. "I found an apartment."

He turned around, his face reddening. "You did what? Why did you do that?"

"We both know this isn't working. I need to think of myself for once. I can't stay here anymore."

"You're never going to make it alone. It's a big world out there, and you don't know anything about it."

I turned away and went upstairs. I sat down on the bed and stared outside at the birch trees and the blue hills beyond. It was a big world out there. Would getting a divorce make anything easier?

Unopened boxes sat on top of the old oak table in my new apartment. This would be my home now—no husband, no children, no dog. I walked through the empty rooms. Conflicted feelings of loss and newness tossed about in my heart. *What was I doing? Two decades of marriage crumbling into a divorce. What would it be like to be a divorced woman, living alone? Would I be happy or miserable? How did it ever come to this?*

I found an excuse to go to the store and pushed the cart up and down unfamiliar aisles, not knowing why I was there or what I wanted to buy. As angry tears slipped down my face, I brushed them away, afraid someone would think I was crazy. Maybe Jim was right when he'd said I'd never make it alone. But I wasn't going back. Somehow, I would make it through this divorce and be better for it.

I bought a new bed, one with no memories. I'd lay in the darkness, unanswered questions swirling in my head. Anxiety and fear filled my sleepless nights. But not remorse.

Slowly, loneliness turned into a feeling of peace. Self-doubt and frustration grew into strength and tenacity. Katy was right: I did get through it, and I'm more than fine. Now, I'm happy. My college diploma hangs on my office wall, and I write against dead-lines. I finally found myself; I know what, and who, I want in my life.

The U-Haul backs slowly out of Pat's driveway and lumbers down the street, Pat's hands steady on the steering wheel. I wave at her. She waves back and turns her head to the road. She'll get through this. She'll be just fine.

—Jodi Henry

For the Birds

Just after her seventy-third birthday, my mother stood in the living room of her new Oregon apartment. Weeks before, in her native Arizona, she'd had a knee replacement, a garage sale, and an epiphany. After fifteen years of marriage, she was leaving my stepfather, Ron.

I was at her newly leased place, helping decide how to decorate the walls. She held up a painting my father had created decades before. "I've missed you," she told the, Picasso-inspired oil, and I wondered how she'd made it through these years without Dad. Before he died, they'd worshipped one another, something I thought all couples did, until I got married and divorced myself.

Now, tension masked her sunny disposition. Mom narrowed her eyes. "Ron was so jealous. He never could stand to see any of your father's artwork."

I started to remind her that now that she was getting a divorce, she was free to display anything she wanted. Before I could say so, chirps and trills sounded from the kitchen.

"That's the bird clock I got for my birthday," she said, gently leaning Dad's painting against a wall.

I poked my head around the corner. On the clock's face, a cardinal perched at the top, followed by a robin, a cedar waxwing, a jay, and several other species. Every hour a different one sings.

Mom, still hobbling from her knee surgery, joined me in the kitchen. She frowned and pointed. "It's three, isn't it?

I checked my watch and nodded.

"That's the problem. At three, the blue jay should call. Instead, we're getting the waxwing. It's driving me nuts. The darn thing's one bird off."

I started to laugh, but then remembered: until the final decree, my mother's surname would be Bird.

She answered as if she'd read my mind. "Your aunt gave it to me. Ron tried to say it was his, just because of his last name. But I won that round."

That round. There'd been trouble for years, but Mom and Ron's split had started almost amicably. Neither could take care of the other any longer. Ron's problems included heart disease, diabetes, and neuropathy. In addition to her bum knee, Mom's balance and fine motor skills had been damaged from a spinal cord injury. The couple decided it was best to go their separate ways. Simple. No fault.

But as they'd divided property and negotiated terms, grudging smiles had dissolved into hateful sneers. Ordinary belongings suddenly became priceless heirlooms. Both sides dug in, not wishing to give the other a hint of satisfaction.

In the midst of the move-in mess, Mom pawed through a box of odds and ends next to the stove. "I know I bought a roll of stamps before I left Scottsdale." She frowned. "I've got to get a letter out to my attorney today. That you-know-what's countersuing. Should I try calling the law office instead?"

You're the mom; you should be dispensing advice, I thought. At her age, Mom wasn't supposed to be starting over. As a new mother, I'd phoned Mom in tears if the baby spit up or got diaper rash. Now I was thirty years into my second marriage, far removed from the dissolution process. Even if I were an expert, talking with Mom about divorce felt downright awkward. I tried to distract her.

I held Dad's painting against the wall above the sofa. "Wouldn't this look fabulous here?"

She tilted her head to one side. "Did I tell you I'm taking back my maiden name?"

I nearly lost my grip on the picture and had to set it down. I hadn't thought of that. What, my father's name, Stoops, wasn't good enough? Okay, I admit I spent my youth trying to get rid of that handle, too. What else about my mother might change?

A year after Dad died, Mom married Ron Bird. I tried to like him. He had not the slightest sense of aesthetics, but he'd retired with plenty of money. He lived at an exclusive golf country club in Scottsdale. She could step out the back door to play a round. Maybe Ron couldn't emulate Dad or Picasso, but my mother would be comfortable and secure.

Wedded bliss was another matter. An hour after the ceremony, the emotional abuse began. He asked if I always dressed like a streetwalker, said women were meant to serve men, and hated my younger sister on sight. He told Mom she looked (expletive) gorgeous right before he demanded she make him another double gin on the rocks.

As the years passed, he belittled Mom in public and in private. When too many drinks slurred his words, his attitude got worse. Soon the Birds had no real friends, and I could see Mom was miserable. I don't think he hit her, but her emotional wounds were plain enough. I found myself loathing Ron and comparing him with my artistic and loving father.

Yet, for fifteen years she put up with his gin-swilling and verbal abuse. At one point he tried to force her to sever ties with our side of the family, which drove her to swallow a bottleful of sleeping pills. She pulled through, but I was so angry I wanted to strangle the guy and be done with it. I wonder how she survived another two years married to him.

Mom sat on the sofa, patting the seat next to her. I followed the cue and sat beside her. She propped one foot on the coffee table and massaged her knee. "Soon as this heals," she said, "I'm going to start dancing again. Have some fun for a change."

I put my arm around her. "After all you've been through, you deserve to be happy." I didn't say I hoped she'd be content with memories of Dad.

She smiled. "Maybe I'll even meet a dancing partner."

My heart speeded up. My mother, dating again? I didn't want to think about it. This was the twenty-first century. Did she know about the dangers?

As a young divorcée during the turbulent, disco seventies, I'd had my share of bad dates. Mom hadn't lectured, but she'd often reminded me of things to beware: hustlers who tried to talk their way into the bedroom; deadbeats looking for someone to support them; men who'd go to great lengths to hide their sketchy pasts, bad credit, or wife and kids. And of course, avoid the abusers. Guess she hadn't seen that one coming.

By now I hoped Mom had learned how to spot a creep. But what if some guy danced his way right into her bank account?

"Mom," I said, "Do you realize how different things are nowadays?"

"What are you talking about?"

I gulped. "I mean, you know, dating, the bar scene, that sort of stuff. You can't be too careful. What if you meet another—"

"Ron?" Her steely gray eyes sparked. "For heaven's sake. I want a dance partner, not another husband. Don't worry about me."

"But I do worry. I couldn't stand to see you hurt again."

Her expression softened. She patted my knee. "I know you're trying to help. But I'm not ready for the old folks' home yet. I've got a lot of living to do." She struggled to her feet and stood back from the sofa again, head tilted to one side. "Hold up the painting one more time, will you?"

I steadied my father's oil against the wall. She nodded her approval. I smiled. My father's painting had waited years to regain its place in Mom's living room.

"So now you'll be a Clark instead of a Bird?" I asked.

"Olé!" She snapped her fingers like a flamenco dancer. "I've always wanted to tango."

We spent a while longer sorting through boxes, deciding where other pictures might look best. When the clock sounded four, we heard a squawk instead of chirping.

Mom pursed her lips. "Hear that? That's the blue jay. But this time it should be the chickadee." She sighed. "I guess it's going to take time to smooth out the bumps."

If she meant life's bumps, I couldn't have agreed more. And I realize that, even after the divorce battles are settled and it's final, I'll need to continue working on letting my mother live the life she desires, not the one I wish for her. She may opt to stay a happy single grandma, or she may team up with a new dance partner.

Later, on my way out the door, I kissed my mother's cheek. "Be back tomorrow," I said. "I'll bring stamps, and I'll tell Brad about fixing your clock."

"Oh yes, the clock," Mom deadpanned. "Just like I'll be when this is all over—one Bird off."

—Linda S. Clare

When the Rubber Band Breaks

A twisted rubber band sends a bamboo airplane soaring—provided it is not overwound. But twist it just one fateful turn too many, and there comes a resounding smack of broken rubber band.

I felt my internal rubber band turning tighter and tighter as I juggled divorce proceedings, job stresses, and mothering challenges. I knew I should do something constructive to lower my stress level, but I had three hurting children to provide for, nurture, and raise. So I just pressed on . . . until the evening my five-year-old refused to come inside when I called for him, dinner was taking too long and my toddler was whining about being hungry, and my seven-year-old stood with the phone in her hand demanding an answer that was more to her liking.

"But she says it's free," Katie wheedled. "I bet her mom would drive me to the meeting."

"No," I said, repeating my earlier answer with a forced calm.

"But all you have to do is drive me to Shelley's house. Her mom will do the rest. Can't I go? Ple-e-ease."

Boing! The rubber band inside me snapped. "I said no!" I screamed.

That brought her brother, Chris, inside, where he joined his two siblings in staring at me with big eyes and dropped jaws.

I am not using the word scream in exaggeration. I did not slightly raise my voice in irritation. My scream sent shockwaves throughout our small apartment. My voice box hurt from the explosion.

"I'm sorry, kids," I said, in immediate remorse.

Three pairs of stressed eyes remained glued on me. *Now what?* their pupils silently asked. I was the parent they depended on.

"I'm putting myself in a time-out," I told them. "I need to calm down."

The worry in their eyes disappeared. They understood this language. I had never put myself in time-out, but I'd put them in time-outs before. Time-out was a consequence for out-of-control behavior. It was a safe place to regain self-control.

"Why don't the three of you set the table for dinner, and we'll eat right after Mommy's time-out is over."

Three heads nodded, and Katie delegated respon-sibilities. I scurried down the hallway to the sanctuary of privacy. After a few minutes of desperate prayer and deep calming breaths, I went out to the kitchen and calmly dispensed hugs and apologies. They were quick to forgive, and we sat down and enjoyed a nice, peace-ful family dinner. We carried on with our normal routine for the rest of the evening. But I knew that I would be making some changes in the near future. I needed to bring down my stress level, somehow.

After the children went to bed, I sat on the couch futon that served as my bed and poured my troubled feelings into a journal. I brainstormed, seeking solu-tions to the endless stress that being a-woman-in-the-process-of-a-divorce entailed.

Over the following days, weeks, and months, I implemented my new strategy: Self-care was now a vital part of my job description as a woman. If I did not take proper care of myself, then everyone I touched would lose—including me. I decided I wanted to be a divorced woman who was creating balance and whole-ness within herself and her family.

Filling the craters inside myself that had been cre-ated by fourteen years of a bad marriage and filling the new holes dug by losing my former identity as a married woman led to an unexpected and excit-ing journey of discovering myself. I grew in new and liberating directions, and I became an explorer, venturing into new territory. Divorce became my opportunity to make a fresh start on becoming who I wanted to be.

I wrote down a detailed list of who I wanted to become as a female, a divorcing woman, a mom, a career woman, a woman of faith, a neighbor, and a citizen. I posted my list on a bulletin board that I hung by my dining table. Reviewing that list daily helped me to focus my efforts and led to a new, better way of living.

One of my new goals was to be a more playful woman. My life history held trauma and abuse that had squashed lightheartedness out of me. Now, I wanted to learn how to enjoy life and cherish it. I began by forcing myself to do one fun thing when my children were visiting their dad. At first, I had to fight the counterproductive "I should be working every second" inner voice and the "you don't deserve fun because you should be grieving your failed marriage" inner chiding. Those guilt-producing messages were wrong. I did need to grieve, but not every second. I needed to work hard, too, but I would work better if I rested now and then.

It wasn't easy, at first, to schedule a picnic for myself in the sunshine or to just go hang out with my brother or to hike a mountain trail or to drop in on a friend for a spontaneous visit. But the benefits were obvious: I felt more relaxed and energetic when my children returned. I felt more alive, in general, and found myself becoming more playful with my children. I began doing things like suggesting we take off our shoes at the park so we could feel the cool dampness of dew-kissed grass. I impulsively would cry out, "Let's race to that tree!" and delight my children by taking off running, or "Let's roll down this hill!" followed by bumpy rolling that was so fun we all decided to do it again.

Being more playful kept growing organically into a new lifestyle. Not only did my children and I benefit, but I noticed that we had an impact on others when we were out in public. At the grocery store, clerks noticed that we were enjoying each other and would give me compliments on my parenting. At the skating rink, other women watched me skate freely with and around my kids. They witnessed my attempt at backwards skating, my falls, laughter, and getting up to try it again. I watched as one brave female soul after another caught my eye and then got up to rent skates for herself. Soon, four of us moms were playing with our children on the rink.

Another stress-reducer that I adopted, and plan never to let go of, was intentionally cultivating a thankful spirit. I became much happier as I wrote down things I was grateful for each day. At first, it was difficult. I was going through lots of pain during the divorce, and my former husband was showing his very worst side during the process. Initially, I challenged myself to record just one good thing each day. When that became easy, I wrote down three a day and then later five. And then I lost track. Recognizing all the nice things people did and said, all the joy I found in nature, and all the growth in my children blessed me tremendously. I realized that my former self had taken too much for granted and focused too much on worries. My new self concentrated on blessings and appreciated others. I liked who I was becoming.

Divorce turned out to be more than an ending. It was the beginning of a new me and an improved mother for my children. It was the beginning of a life that I embrace wholeheartedly and enjoy tremendously. I remember telling myself shortly after I filed divorce papers that I might never be happy again but that I needed to take care of my children's needs for a safe and secure home. I was right about needing to take care of their needs. I was wrong about never being happy again. By learning to take care of my own needs, I found happiness, joy, and peace. The divorce that had nearly broken me more than a decade ago was, in reality, the start of a life that I now cherish.

—Tanya T. Warrington

The Passage

I struggled with the decision of whether to have children. On long walks, I would make mental lists of the pros and cons of having children, but as soon as I found myself back home, facing the door to our apartment, I would slam into the fear that I'd been pushing aside all day. I wanted children but was terrified of ending up a single mom, like my mother.

The fear would not be tamed by logic, though I tried. I argued a strong case for why my parents had separated and why my husband and I would not. We had already been married eight years, and I didn't see any signs of instability. If anything, we were a little too set in our routines: the unvarying weekday and Saturday morning workouts at the gym, the evenings spent reading books or talking about my husband's business, the quiet dinners in elegant restaurants.

I longed for children for reasons I could not explain. Also—though I kept this from my husband—I wanted children because I believed they would throw us off the narrowing track to predictability and dry perfectionism. But I chose motherhood warily, still believing that having children and then separating would be one of the worst things that could possibly happen in my life.

My husband and I planned to have two children, eighteen months apart. With the unsettling precision that marked so much of our relationship, we had two children, eighteen months and five days apart. Those plump, beautiful babies did, indeed, disrupt our routines with their raw emotions, toothless smiles, and insistent needs. I now had all the change and spontaneity I could have wanted, but change is unpredictable. Though I saw it coming, I could only guess where it was going.

Now when I faced that door to our apartment I no longer worried about being a single mom. For the first year, I struggled to carry my son in a heavy car seat, thinking only of the moment when I could put him down safely. Then I worried about the wide spaces between the stair railings. Then, I was holding both my toddler's hand and my infant daughter in a car seat and plastic mesh covered the railings.

I was so close to my boy and girl that sometimes it seemed skin was the only thing that separated us. In stark contrast to this intimacy between my children and me, I began to notice how many boundaries lay between my husband and me. Before babies, I had seen harmony in our highly structured marital dance. Now, though, a pattern of suppression revealed itself.

"Conversations that begin with 'I feel' don't work for me," my husband announced. "I'm only interested in solid, substantiated facts." He did not trust me with any decision more complicated than the timing of a diaper change. He was furious when he returned from a business trip to find I had moved several pictures on the walls. He accused me of being "out of my *#%@*ing* mind" when I bought my daughter a pair of inexpensive but well-made leather sandals that happened to have a gold-colored finish.

Later that day as he filmed the children at play, I felt a moment of panic when the camera swept across me on its way to zoom in on them. I hoped it wasn't switched on. I was suddenly unreasonably sure that, if I saw myself on film, I would see that my soul was missing.

Our part-time nanny smiled broadly into the camera.

A nineteen-year old high school graduate from Idaho with no father to speak of, she was in awe of my husband's English accent, athletic build, and relative affluence. He proudly told me that she thought he was the ideal man, but that she wasn't on the pill. Something stirred in my spineless, save-the-marriage-at-any-cost depths.

"Even talking about birth control with our nanny seems inappropriate to me," I said.

He said I was too closed-minded. He, being open-minded, had a much better solution for the discontent in our marriage: a *ménage a trois*. Such an arrangement would enable him to give unfettered expression to his true, polygamous, alpha-male nature as sexual partner to multiple women and adoring father to his children. It was necessary, natural, and optimal, and I would be narrow-minded, selfish, and sexually repressed if I couldn't see how perfect it was for him. For us, that is.

It was a shock. I didn't know what I should do next—but my friends did. When that nameless feeling stirring in my gut backed them up, I followed their directions as if they were a guard rail gleaming through the fog.

"Fire her," my friend Judith had said, the smoke from her cigarette wreathing her grey hair. "Write her final check; don't add in any severance money.

Hold the check so she can see it while you're talking, that way she'll hear you out. Practice first, so you tell her everything you need to say. Leave nothing to regret."

"And as for him . . . " she leaned forward and tipped the long tail of ash into a saucer, pulling herself back from telling me what to do. "Some people can live with infidelity. Others can't. You'll know what's right for you."

Two strained and silent days after my conversation with my husband, I slipped out of the apartment while he and the children were having breakfast. I met the nanny at the foot of the stairs and told her in a well-rehearsed and calm speech that I was firing her and why. I handed her the check I'd been holding in her sight and took back her keys.

I walked back up the concrete stairs, dizzy at the sudden shift of power, feeling strong and afraid, as alive as new skin when it sheds the scab. I had just defied the pattern of our entire marriage, and I did not believe it would survive. As my trembling fingers aimed the key at the lock, the gesture triggered a memory of all those times when I had stood at this very same door and felt waves of fear clenching my gut at the thought of being a single mom. Now, despite all that worrying and analysis and planning, it was coming true. It was happening to me.

The fear washed over me, larger than ever, but for the last time. So here it was: the unthinkable. But it wasn't what I had imagined. Suddenly, I knew that divorce would not be a nightmare. It would be nothing more or less than daily life with my children, only without another grownup there for support and affection. It would, in fact, be much the same as the life I was living now. But I would have my soul back, and with it, a life once again vibrant with possibility.

I couldn't say for certain what it would be like on the other side of the door, but on this side, I felt my feet strong in my boots, my heart pounding in my chest, and my hand suddenly steady on the door knob, ready now. I stepped over the threshold, feeling my feet connect with the ground, strode into our apartment, and tossed the ex-nanny's keys onto the table.

—Anne-Christine Strugnell

With This Ring

I placed the wedding set on my finger, took a deep breath, and entered the most expensive jewelry store in town. The once-familiar bands now felt tight and restrictive on my finger.

"I'm here for an appraisal," I said, removing my wedding set and placing the symbol of eternal love in the clerk's palm.

He brought the ring to his eye and measured the diamond. "Has this been in the family long?"

I nodded and swallowed the lump forming in my throat. "Several years," I said as he placed the ring my ex-husband had given me twelve years ago on the scales and typed the weight into the computer.

I willed my mind to erase the way the engagement ring had looked in the velvet maroon colored box and the excitement I had felt when my ex-husband proposed. I needed to forget the way his eyes had sparkled with love and the promise of forever. I begged my brain to forget the feel of his fingers, warm and steady, as they placed the band on my finger and sealed his promise with a kiss. I tried to steady my quivering chin while the appraiser placed a value on my memories.

"You should insure the set for five-thousand dollars," the appraiser said as he reached for an insurance brochure. "Our company offers several affordable insurance packages for a nominal fee."

I cleared my throat. "I'm sorry," I said. "I need the appraised value to sell the rings, not to insure them."

He removed his glasses and nodded slightly. He understood.

I had kept the wedding rings after my divorce a year earlier, hoping to pass them down to my daughter. But being a single parent had proven more difficult than I'd expected, as was the decision to sell the rings.

I leaned forward and placed my shaking hands on the desk, "I'm a little afraid to advertise the rings on eBay," I said. "Please tell me how I can sell the jewelry without compromising my safety."

The appraiser launched into a discussion about the dangers of selling jewelry to strangers, and I agreed. The last thing I wanted was to be mugged by someone more desperate than me.

"The safest way to sell the wedding set is to have an estate house sell them for you on consignment," he said. "An estate house could get you half the appraised value. But I need to be clear, five-thousand dollars is the insured replacement value. You can expect to receive twenty-five-hundred dollars when you sell the wedding set on consignment. Not a penny more."

Braces for my daughter were going to cost at least that.

"You chose a good time to sell," he continued. "The holidays are approaching. In fact, I have a buyer who is interested in a diamond this size. The stone will be removed and the gold melted down. Something new and beautiful will be made from your wedding set."

I thought I was going to vomit. The last valuable item that remained from my failed marriage was going to the chop shop. I glanced toward the scale.

I suppressed the urge to grab the rings and bolt for the door.

The appraiser must have sensed my reluctance. He removed the rings from the scale and extended them to me. "Give it some thought," he said while pressing his card into my hand. "Give me a call when you are serious about selling."

I looked at him and willed away the tears. My voice faltered as I spoke. "The rings haven't been worn in years. It's time they found a new home."

I signed the consignment agreement and fled.

As I drove home in my ten-year-old car, I tried to curb my emotions. Why was I so upset about selling a piece of jewelry that no longer held any meaning? It's not like I want to go back to a loveless marriage.

But the rings had meant something, at least to me. Having to sell my wedding rings confirmed that I had failed at my marriage. It also confirmed what I had suspected: I had been taken for a fool. I had believed that this man loved and would cherish me. Most of all, I believed that he would honor our marriage vows. The wedding rings were supposed to be a constant reminder of his promise. Weren't they?

I'd sacrificed a lot when I divorced my ex-husband more than a year ago. As if downsizing from a five-bedroom house to a two-bedroom apartment wasn't enough, I also lost many friends. Divorce has a way of doing that; friends either take sides or disappear altogether. The social circle I once thrived in now whispered behind my back. The charities to which I had given so freely had stopped calling because they really didn't need my volunteer time; they wanted my money, which I no longer had to give.

While I tumbled far financially, my ex-husband slept soundly in the comfort of our bed . . . with her, the woman he'd had on the side for years. The woman I begged him to give up in order to save our marriage. The woman who efficiently replaced me, so he wouldn't have to spend one night alone. As I waited for the traffic light to change I wondered, *How had it been possible for a marriage certificate made of thin paper to divide my life between poverty and prosperity?*

The pity party began to subside and anger began to build, bringing with it the other memories I had long suppressed. Memories of his graphic e-mails and online dating ads I'd discovered after years of marriage flashed hot before me. Recollections of hours I spent coiled in the fetal position, clinging to the phone, while girlfriends begged me to leave him. Flashbacks of the other women he had in every town he visited. Nuances of the neurosis I felt every time he left for a business trip. How could I have forgotten the loneliness the pangs of self-doubt I had felt?

My mind replayed a scene when I had walked into our bedroom and overheard him whispering on his cell: "My wife doesn't know what sexy is, but you always knew." How could I have possibly forgotten those words?

"Damn it, I am sexy!" I yelled over the noise of the car engine as I unleashed my frustration on the steering wheel.

And the anger felt good. The anger burned away the sentimental cobwebs of my nuptials. The anger destroyed the good times, reminding me that his lies and deceit never equaled love. The anger cleansed my soul and focused my thoughts. The anger also reminded me of what was important—me. In the struggle to save my marriage and then later survive the divorce, I had forgotten about taking care of me.

A horn sounded, jolting me into the present. The light had turned green, time to move forward. As I drove my rattletrap car, I tilted my chin high as if my ride were a shiny new Mercedes, just like the one he'd bought her for her birthday.

I left the last remaining part of who I'd been at that traffic light. I had nothing but the road and my future ahead of me. A smile formed on my once-quivering lips.

"I am smart," I whispered. Smart enough to sell the last piece of us to a complete stranger. Smart enough to stop looking back and to start looking forward.

With this newfound confidence I strutted into Victoria's Secret and bought something sexy. And, darling, let me tell you, I made it look good!

—*Renea Winchester*

Playing with Fire

I am a firefighter.

That reality occurred to me on my way to work as I practiced what I would say to the bank. Paul's check had bounced, overdrawing our joint account, the same account, good God, with which I had bought the cashier's check for the refinance of our home.

It had been four months since Paul had left, so angry and determined. Four months since I'd collapsed to the floor, too stunned to remain standing.

Our story was the classic one, only it was an eleven-year itch instead of seven and my husband's "Marilyn" was a classmate in his quest for an engineering degree. Not to worry, though, they were just friends, just good friends. Actually, that may have been true. I don't really know. I only know that he preferred her company, her laugh; that he could share a beer with her without her scrunching up her nose at the smell; that it was her shoulder he ran to for consolation after he left.

Weeks later, when practical financial needs crowded in on my grief, I'd suggested we refinance to reduce the mortgage bill I was now paying on my own. He said he'd help now that he was working again. I'd said thank you. After all, the house was still half his, though he no longer called it home.

The teller hadn't wanted to immediately credit Paul's check to my account, because it was drawn on a different bank (a symbol of his newfound freedom). But I'd asked nicely and with a note of desperation in my eyes, and since I was a good customer—a former employee, no less—it was done. Of course, it hadn't hurt that the assistant manager—Warren, a former friend and colleague, in that order—had given me an endorsing pat on the back while I stood at the teller's station. But then the check had bounced because Paul had not deposited the funds in time. Now, my good name and Warren's good authority would be in question. It was five-hundred dollars, after all.

I called the bank right at nine. Warren was happy to hear from me; there was that, at least. I explained and apologized; then asked how his job was going ... gosh, we hadn't had time to chat the other day. He said the bounced check was not a biggie, to just replace it on Monday with a better one. I laughed, relieved. We exchanged "see you laters," and I set the phone down gently on its cradle. I leaned back in my office chair, finally daring to close my eyes and sigh. Sweet relief. Another problem quenched.

It was a small fire, all things considered. I'd put out much worse in the years I'd been married to Paul. Some caused only minor damage, like when he forgot to pay his motorcycle insurance. We even laughed about that one. "Hey, honey," I teased, holding up the cancellation note that had just arrived in the mail. "Did you know you were riding without insurance?"

"Really?" he grinned. "Good thing I didn't have an accident."

Other fires were more intense: friends' hurt feelings when one of Paul's sarcastic quips cut too deep or when one of his mood swings flared up and resulted in a disciplinary action at work. I even paved the way for his entry into the university when the bureaucratic red tape left him tangled in frustration and unable to move academically. I strolled into the admissions department, paid a polite smile and thank you, nothing really, and picked up the paperwork. Within a few weeks, he was in and I had passed my first test toward my own PhT degree: Putting husband Through.

So, when he told me the other day that he'd lost a measure of trust in me, I couldn't believe it. The man who left me to search for his soul in the arms of another woman . . . *he* couldn't trust *me*?

"That's right," he said and went on to describe a scene we had played out months before, an afternoon when we had met to discuss all the usual gooey details associated with separation. I remembered well that day, that moment. My heart was still raw from his recent and abrupt departure, a pain without ebb punctuated by the distracting fear of facing life on my own. He, in contrast, had been both proud and defensive, asserting his plans for independence. I'd asked—okay, fine, I begged him—to reconsider, to try working it out. Nope, his sights were set on adventure the hell away from here. He set out a calculator and a blank writing pad on our dining room table.

"All right," he said. "Let's get to it."

Feeling numb, a recent defense mechanism, I had reached into my bag and pulled out pages of detailed listings: assets and liabilities, legal responsibilities to consider, options for an absent husband. Paul stared at the growing stack in surprise, a new expression for him, but his wide eyes quickly creased with anger. I saw the transformation, so familiar; I started to cry.

Distraught with the results of my mistake, I tried to convince him of an option not listed: reconciliation. "Please . . ." But he had stopped listening and left soon after, slamming the front door on his way out to serve as his final word.

That's why, he said, he couldn't fully trust me any more. He never wanted to be in that position again. "Do you know how stupid I felt when you pulled out all those papers, while I sat there with just a blank notepad?"

I didn't answer. I just looked at his annoyed, angry face, and suddenly I felt powerful, strong, and amazingly calm. I realized that I had started the fire this time—and I wasn't about to put it out. Ever again.

—*Barbara Neal Varma*

The names in this story have been changed to respect the privacy of those involved.

Happy Father's Day, Mommy

Like a rumbling tidal wave, Father's Day was quickly approaching. Rose and I scanned the greeting card aisle in Walgreens, looking for just the right one. Hmm, I didn't see any that read, "Where the heck are you?" So I let my daughter decide. At five years old, Rose was innocent, beautiful, and totally unaware that her father was gone like the wind, his whereabouts unknown.

I hadn't heard from my ex-husband in nearly a year, when he'd told me there was work waiting for him in Key West and that he'd be in touch once he got settled. Key West was only hours away, and he promised he would visit Rose as much as possible. I didn't really believe him; by then, I had learned not to expect anything from him. I'd often told him that it was easier to be pleasantly surprised than to be sadly disappointed. Ever since our divorce four years earlier, he'd been nothing but consistent with his disappointments. And since he couldn't hold down a job, child support was nonexistent.

"Found one!" Rose said, holding up a giant card with a picture of a monkey on the front.

"That's perfect!" I said.

She giggled as she read the caption, "I'm bananas over you, Dad!"

I smiled and took the card, thinking, *Great. $3.95 for a card going to nowhere.*

Later that night, Rose colored a picture to put inside the card. It was of a house and a rainbow. No people, just green grass, an orange house, and three arced bands of blue, purple, and yellow.

"Where is everyone?" I asked.

"Oh, they're inside the house," Rose said.

"Doing what?"

She sighed as if I should know this already. "Watching TV!"

"But they're missing out on such a beautiful, colorful sky," I said.

"Yeah, I guess."

She then carefully folded the picture and put it inside the card. I helped her put it all in the envelope and let her lick it close. "Yuck," she said. I nodded. "It would be better if it tasted like bubble gum, huh?" She giggled.

"Mommy, can I write the address on the envelope?"

Address? I panicked. What address? "Um, okay," I said, handing her a pen. "It's one-two-three Sunshine Street."

A minute later, she slammed the pen down. "I messed up!"

I scooted my chair next to her and looked at the envelope. She had written the three backwards. "It's okay, pumpkin. The mail person will know it's a three."

"No!" She picked up a purple crayon and began scribbling all over the envelope. She ground the crayon into the envelope, tossed it aside, then picked up the blue one and started scribbling again.

"Rose Veronica!" I cried.

She looked at me, her eyes wide and darting, then jumped out of the chair and ran upstairs.

I wanted to follow her, to find out what had caused this sudden explosion. But something told me to let her go, to give her time, let her breathe. I looked down at the envelope. She had scribbled so hard there were small chunks of purple and blue spread out like a rocky landscape. I thought about her father, David. He always seemed to bring out the worst in people, and now it appeared he was doing it from hundreds of miles away.

I waited a few more minutes before I walked upstairs. Her door was closed. A note on the door in her handwriting read "NOK!" I knocked. She didn't answer, but I could hear her crying. As I turned around to leave, I heard her call for me.

I found her sitting up in her bed, hugging her knees. She looked at me with big brown eyes rimmed in red. "Why doesn't Daddy call me?" she whispered.

I sat beside her on the SpongeBob SquarePants comforter I had bought for her birthday only a few months before. I stroked her thick brown hair, pushing strands behind her ears. I hated such questions. It required me to lie to my own child. I mean, how could I tell her that her daddy was probably in jail for a bar fight at Sloppy Joe's, or worse, living with the derelicts on Smather's Beach? How could I tell her that her father was a hopeless alcoholic and that I was happy he didn't call her? Ever.

"He's probably just really busy at his new job," I said.

"No, he's not! I don't want to send him a card! I hate him!"

I sat on the edge of the bed. "You don't hate your daddy, and your daddy doesn't hate you, sweetie. Remember that Jesus teaches us to love others, to forgive others who have hurt us." I took her hand and held it to her heart. "Feel that? It's warm, isn't it?"

She nodded.

"That is where God lives, and he keeps his key in your heart. That very special key opens your heart to love and forgiveness. Oh, Rosie, your father loves you very much."

"No, he doesn't!"

I stood up and walked over to the small pink bookcase in the corner of her room. On the top sat her baby book, a white cloth-covered photo album adorned with pink ribbons and a pattern of roses. I took it over to the bed and sat close to Rose, so our laps could share the album. The first page contained her sonogram pictures, black-and-white images of a floating figure, appearing to be sucking her thumb. The next page had pictures of Rose at two days old, her tiny head lopping to one side, black button eyes wide with wonder, her father and grandfather smiling in unison, each holding a small part of her. I proceeded to show her all of the pictures, saying nothing. When we got to the picture of her father holding her against a background of the Atlantic, taken on a windy and cloudy day, she had stopped crying and had instead started to smile.

I put away the photo album. A good kind of quiet filled the room, like the quiet after a spring rain, when the only sound is the drip, drip of the water falling off the eaves of an overhanging porch.

"Do you want me to find another envelope for that card?" I asked her.

She touched her chest, as if looking for that key. "Okay," she said. "That's fine."

I decided then that if this hurt, confused, little girl could forgive her father, then so could I. That night, I called his brother, found out that he was, indeed, in jail in Key West, and got the address. I mailed the card the very next day.

The Friday before Father's Day, after a long day (heck, week!) at work, I picked up Rose from after-school care. She smiled and held up a paper the color of cotton candy, waving it around like a banner. "Mommy! I've got something for you!"

After signing her out, we stood in the school's parking lot, our hands locked, as I read what she had written on that colorful banner.

~ My Mom

My mom is the best mom in the world! She plays with me all the time. We like to howl at the moon when it is full. She makes the best ketchup sandwiches. I love her so much! She is my Mommy-Daddy.

"Happy Father's Day, Mommy," she said and squeezed my hand.

I squeezed back, feeling the plump softness of her tiny hand. And at that precise moment, I felt something pass between us, as if a small key crossed from her hand into mine.

—Natalie Sullivan

The Cheese Stands Alone

I never wanted to be the cheese; I never wanted to stand alone. My desire to be married started at four, when we played the game The Farmer in the Dell at day care. Perhaps I took things too seriously at such a young age, but my desire for love and approval was great. One could argue that bribing Johnny with half of my Hostess cupcake to pick me as the wife was a little desperate, but then, I have always been goal-oriented and incredibly focused.

I thought I'd found the perfect man for me at age six. I got fairly serious with a boy named Rex. I have no regrets for taking that dare and kissing him on the cheek in the pantry. Even though my family eventually moved to another town, for years I held out hope we would someday be reunited at the altar.

As a child I spent endless days acting out romance with my Ken and Barbie dolls. My grandmother sewed

Barbie a fantastic satin wedding dress, complete with bridal cap and veil. The matching white plastic pumps cost me half of my allowance, but, like any shoe worth having, I considered them a great investment. Ken, unfortunately, had only jeans and a grungy work shirt to wear to the lavish nuptials I continuously threw for the lucky couple. He also attended all the mock weddings barefoot, often with smudge on his vinyl toes. Ken's lack of good grooming and fashion sense never bothered me. In retrospect, he was a harbinger for the type of the guys I would often fall for later in life.

It only got worse. In junior high I lost any math skills I might have acquired up to age twelve as well as any brain cells that might have been earmarked for science. With the exception of good literature, including romance novels, of course, all my concentration went to *boys*! It's all we girls talked about in our spare time. The burning daily questions and observations included: "Have you been asked to the dance? I think Kevin likes you; do you want me to ask Mark to ask him if he does? Do you want to come to my sleepover? We're going to play Mystery Date." My obsession with the male gender grew as fast as mold on cheese.

Pathetically, it wasn't until I was thirty-five and mother to a boy in the seventh grade that my big epiphany about males occurred. I overheard my son talking on the phone to a friend. Lo and behold, it wasn't about girls! They talked about nachos, trading cards, and episodes of *The Simpsons*. Indeed, girls were about the last thing they ever talked about. Had I known this in junior high, I might possibly be a well-paid chemist or the CEO of a Fortune 500 company today.

Continuing on down the road of life (I'm going to pretend high school didn't happen. I can do this; I am good at playing pretend!), I managed to go to college and read Betty Friedan, Germaine Greer, and Gloria Steinem. But let's face it: it's hard to meet guys in a Women's Studies class. The History of Sports, Weight Training, and even American Cinema Film Noir class proved fertile ground for possible partner prowling. And yet, despite attending five colleges over seven years, and dating a lot of buff film buffs, I ended up meeting my would-be husband at a bar. I was a waitress, although I thought I was definitely on track to being a world-famous reporter for *National Geographic*. Ladies, I will tell you this: it is never a good sign when you meet your future husband while serving him beer and corn nuts.

But never mind that hindsight cynicism. I was *in love* and eventually had a nice wedding ring with a diamond that sparkled. It sparkled as I bleached socks and burped babies. (By the way, I am not a shallow person, and I don't think it's the size of the rock that matters, but rather, whether it holds up over time.) It sparkled as we went through the love, the marriage, and the baby carriage routine. It sparkled all the way up to that day when my marriage was officially over, and possibly it is still sparkling at the bottom of my jewelry box.

The fact of the matter remains that after ten years of marriage I found myself being the cheese. It had come my time to stand alone. I found this completely terrifying, yet at the same time curiously liberating. At one time I might have perceived myself a loser in the game of life; however, I discovered I played a mean game of solitaire. Yes, at times I really longed for someone to come in and play house with me or at least help me mow the lawn. (Okay, I did end up dating a landscaper for a while. No regrets! He was sweet, and I had a big lawn.) I won't pretend there weren't times I felt sad and lonely. But standing alone turned out to have some silver linings. I developed sturdy legs that were used for carrying my own weight and not primarily for flirting. I taught myself how to juggle, which takes immense concentration and is better for you than drinking. I showered myself with a little attention and approval for a change and didn't leave the towel on the floor afterward.

Yes, I've learned that it's really okay not to be "the wife." And I have hope the new generation of girls knows that the Dell is a really great computer but is no place to meet a man.

—*Elizabeth King Gerlach*

Guess Who's Coming to Dinner

Thanksgiving has always been our family's favorite holiday for get-togethers, but the one thing I was not thankful for last year was the fact that my ex-husband was still one of my brother-in-law's favorite drinking buddies. I knew Patrick would be invited to join in the festivities. For my sister's sake, I would keep the peace. I would paste on a smile and act nonchalant, pretending I didn't mind his company. It would all be oh so civil. The drunken temper fits and infidelity were just part of a whispered past no one mentioned.

The setting sun was low enough to peek under the windshield visor of my Taurus as I backed off the gravel and parked at the edge of my sister's driveway. The kids leaped out of the car and ran toward the backyard before I could even shut off the engine.

I was in no such hurry. Plodding around to the passenger side, I took my time opening the door, gathering up my purse, and retrieving the huge pot of mashed potatoes from the passenger seat. Then I slammed the door and leaned against the fender to compose myself. As I walked around the house to the backyard, I could already hear Patrick's low laugh.

Our Thanksgiving feast was held in the game room, which was a converted shop building located behind the main house. My sister and her husband had renovated the shop and added a wood stove, games, and a refrigerator to keep the beer and other refreshments cold.

I trudged across the thick lawn, took a deep breath, and reached for the heavy wooden door. My kids, who had rushed to the backyard ahead of me to greet the chickens and ducks, spotted me and rushed over, so we could all go in together. I braced myself before stepping into the room, but nothing could have prepared me for what was behind that door.

Patrick was not playing pool with the rest of the men across the room. To my surprise, he was at the food table set up just inside the door, standing behind a woman I'd never met, his hands resting on her shoulders. As I stepped inside and closed the door, he leaned down to whisper in her ear. The woman was striking. Her salon-styled hair and perfect make-up complemented beautiful polished fingernails.

I set my potatoes on the table and shoved my unmanicured hands deep into the pockets of my sweat jacket. Sitting down at the table, I said hello to my sister and grandma, and then waited to be introduced. First, though, my kids rushed around the table and hugged Patrick from three sides. Finally, he turned to me.

"Miss Tisha," he flashed his best Mr. Charming smile. Ten years ago, his soft brown eyes would have melted my heart, but I fought that urge now. "I want you to meet my very special friend. This is Lindsey."

Lindsey smiled shyly and extended her hand, "Hi, Tisha. I've heard a lot about you."

"Not all bad, I hope," I answered.

"Oh, of course not," Patrick purred. "I only brag about you, wifey."

"Ex," I hissed, but he did not hear me as he grabbed a beer and headed to the pool table.

"It's nice to meet you," Lindsey blushed and glanced after Patrick.

"It's nice to meet you too, Lindsey," I smiled in return and moved to sit down across the table from her. She barely looked at me. "Don't worry," I assured her. "I'm harmless."

She laughed then, and we sat at the table with the rest of the women, gossiping and watching the kids play. As much as I wanted to hate her, Lindsey was graceful and charming. As we talked, I began to question myself. *He had been so attentive to her. How come he never treated me that well? Was she prettier or somehow better than me? She seemed to keep his interest. Why did he cheat on me?*

Sitting there with no date of my own, I wondered what I had to be thankful for this year. The shadow of depression lasted only a moment, though, as I listened to my kids' laughter and watched Patrick become increasingly more drunk and belligerent as the evening went on. I was missing nothing. And I was ever so thankful to no longer be married to a dysfunctional drunk.

Patrick and Lindsey also came to the family Christmas party together. Lindsey wore a sleek red and green dress. Her hair was styled, and her nails were manicured. She had talked Patrick into getting his hair styled and frosted as well.

"Lindsey, you're absolutely glowing!" my sister swooned when Lindsey joined us in the kitchen.

Lindsey's cheeks reddened as she grinned and whispered, "I'm going to have a baby."

My sister shrieked, and I almost dropped a full bowl of salad. Lindsey was giving Patrick a child of his own, the one thing I could never have given him.

I had my tubes tied the day after my last child was born, years before I met Patrick. Though we could not have kids together, when we married he had gained three stepchildren. He said that was just as good. He must have changed his mind.

I boiled inside watching him treat Lindsey like a princess. Once she was settled on the couch, he brought her a plate of food. Even when Patrick was hanging out with the guys, he gazed at her lovingly from across the room.

Imagine my shock later in the day when I found Lindsey crying in the hallway. Her face was buried in the corner as she sobbed, so she didn't hear or see me approach.

I gently tapped her on the shoulder. "What's wrong?"

Startled, she hurried to wipe away tears. "Oh, Tisha, please don't tell Patrick you saw this. He would be so upset with me."

"What's wrong?" I repeated in a lower voice.

Lindsey just looked at the ground, but when I asked if it was about Patrick, she nodded her head.

"You know, if anyone understands the spot you're in, it's me." I wiped away a few of her tears. "Come on, let's go for a walk."

I asked my sister to watch the kids. Then Lindsey and I stepped outside and headed down the driveway. She walked in silence for a few minutes.

"Lindsey, my life with Patrick was more than a little rocky," I started the conversation. "I know it looks like we are friends now, but our relationship is not as lighthearted as it looks. He can be a hard man to live with."

She stopped and looked long at me, then burst into tears. "It's horrible!" she blurted out between sobs. "He drinks himself to sleep every night. And since I became pregnant, he acts like he doesn't want to touch me. He's out late at night, and I am beginning to think he is . . ." She started to cry louder.

"Cheating on you?" I finished the sentence.

She nodded, and I put my arm around her shoulder. Suddenly, instead of resenting her for having what I lost, I wanted to shield her from the same nightmare I had survived. Maybe divorce would not ruin my life. For the first time, I felt validated in my decision to leave Patrick.

Earlier this year Lindsey gave birth to a healthy, eight-pound baby boy, but she and Patrick are not together any more. He got arrested a couple of times for drunk driving and landed himself in jail.

Patrick and I do not talk much any more, either, but Lindsey and I have found we have much in common. I invited her to Thanksgiving. I have found something new to be thankful for this year. Out of a marriage that turned to dirt sprouted a new friendship . . . and a new life.

—Tisha R. Harris

Can I Have My Town Back?

We open a self-help book, and it tells us that women give too much. We give it all, and often the resentment of all that giving, when we don't feel enough coming back to us, is what breaks up our marriages. In my case, I gave my town away, and now, twenty-five years later, I want it back.

It wasn't resentment that drove me out of my marriage and out of town. It was more like triumph. I had an extremely ambitious husband. He was an assistant U.S. Attorney and a successful mountain climber, preparing to lead an expedition to the summit of dangerous Mt. McKinley in Alaska. He wasn't home very much, that was true. And there were no children. But I was busy, too, with a job as a bank executive and working on an MBA at a local private university. I was successful enough to want freedom, so I didn't mind giving it up, or so I thought at the time. I was so generous I was willing to give up my two residences, a condo on Lake Union and a house on the banks of the Skykomish River at the base of Stevens Pass, along with everything those two residences represented: my home, my land, my career, and the comfort of a companionable marriage.

Being a brilliant lawyer, my husband was able to convince me not to hire one. It was not a messy separation; we didn't fight. I filed the divorce papers the day after I found him with another woman in our bed.

I was only thirty years old when I spread my wings and flew away to find my dream, my true happiness, the star in my heart and soul. I didn't find it easily or soon, but eventually I wanted it enough to make it become a reality.

First, I left Seattle to stay with my parents in Los Angeles for a few months, and then packed my Toyota with all my possessions and my three month-old golden retriever, Casey, and headed east. I drove across the heartland of my country, until we reached its capital in Washington, D.C., and then south, to Virginia. I had lived in Virginia before, graduating from a small women's college near Roanoke before my marriage to the gifted young lawyer. After our divorce, several busy years doing graduate studies in Charlottesville were followed by more traveling, more searching for that elusive happiness, that star missing from my heart. I searched in Europe, in Mexico, in Guatemala, in a lovely Southern California beach town, and finally back in Mexico, still accompanied by my faithful canine companion, Casey.

Mexico became my new home. I was captivated by the sunny friendliness of the county, the simple happiness of the people, and the relaxed way of life. I bought land with a view and built a house. I taught English in the local schools.

And Mexico gave me my star. When I was thirty-eight I gave birth to my daughter, Sarah. It didn't matter that her father was a cute young American I met in a Mexican beach town who would never be my husband nor ever be present as a father for Sarah. My dream was to have a strong, intelligent child, and Sarah was all I ever dreamt of and more. She grew up in Mexico to be fluent in Spanish and English, an accomplished horsewoman by age ten, a happy child, and then a beautiful young woman whose turn it was to fly herself. After graduating from high school in Guadalajara last spring, she left Mexico to attend New York University in New York City, and found herself happily settled in that bustling academic community.

With my daughter recently gone, I know there's something missing in my peaceful life in Mexico, and it's not her. I'm happy she's where she should be, leading a productive and rewarding life. I've let her go, and I now have time to reflect and perhaps to travel. My elderly relatives in Seattle are begging me to visit them. I've visited only once, when Sarah was twelve, for a brief summer stay. I haven't wanted to go back. Seattle wasn't mine, anymore, because I gave it away with my marriage and my two residences and my career.

But that's not true, I now tell myself. I do want my town back. These days in Mexico, the summer rain of the tropics is making me so restless. I want to stand in the rain under those magnificent Douglas firs of the Pacific Northwest, to smell the trees and the earth, and to experience the deep-in-my-soul knowledge that my grandfather and his grandfather were born and died and are buried here. I was too generous, I tell myself. I shouldn't have given it away so easily. I want it back, if only for a short visit, if only for a place in my heart to always treasure, so I can't lose it again.

It's so easy to get it back. I go online and book a round-trip ticket from Guadalajara to Seattle for less than $450, a real bargain! In less than a month I will be there, in my grandmother's house, and it will be mine.

I often ask myself if I was wrong to be so generous to my ex-husband, to walk away and give him
everything. I ask if that feminine open-hearted gen-
erosity, that virtue our mothers taught us, is ever a
mistake. I look out the window of my own beautiful
Mexican house upon a sunny palm-filled landscape
filled with the sounds of Mexican children laughing
in the streets. My daughter's message pops up on my
computer screen, telling me of her writing and media
classes. She sends photos of herself, long blond hair
flying through New York streets. In that moment I
know that when I gave away my town I began to find
my dream. And my town is still there, waiting for my
return.

—*Elizabeth Sellars*

Snow Day

It had snowed overnight, but I didn't have time to admire the drifting flakes or enjoy the white lawn in front of my rented townhouse. Instead, I rushed to ready my young sons for the sitter and school, prepare myself for work, and make sure we all had something hot in our stomachs before meeting the cold world outside.

Once the boys were dressed and sitting at the kitchen table with breakfast in front of them, I sprinted up the stairs to choose an appropriate outfit, fix my hair, and apply mascara for another day at the advertising agency where I worked as a secretary. While I whipped myself together, I gulped my own breakfast: a tepid cup of tea.

Finally, we bundled up, matching mittens and moon boots to six-year-old and four-year-old fingers and feet, and loaded down with school work assembled in backpacks and lunches tucked into cartooned boxes, we stomped through the snow to the car. The boys, snow drunk, kicked the powder with their boots and laughed clouds into the cold air, while I pulled car keys from the purse slung over my shoulder.

Mike and Tim giggled behind their mittens as I tried, again and again, to fit the key in the lock. It kept slipping and wouldn't fit inside. A clear, frozen glaze covered the keyhole, and no amount of picking at the ice would release it. We would not be going anywhere until I boiled a kettle of water to unfreeze the lock. And that would make me late for work. Again.

I swore, stemming tears of frustration with angry curses. Today, of all days, when slick roads would force me to take extra travel time, I was wasting precious minutes on this stupid bit of bad luck. The boys had stopped laughing.

"Sorry, Mommy," Mike said as we trudged back to the apartment.

"It's not your fault," I said, before the tone of his voice had a chance to sink in. "Is it?" I added.

"We thought we could stay home today. Like a snow day. We could all be cozy together, like we used to."

He meant when I'd been a stay-at-home-mom, before the divorce.

"So you froze the lock?"

By then, we were in the apartment, and Tim, my youngest, was unzipping his jacket. He was always too warm, and we fought a daily battle just to get him to wear socks.

"I helped," Tim said. "It was easy."

"We poured water on the lock, and it froze really fast," Mike said, but the wonder and gladness of surprising me seeped quickly from his voice. Delight wiped clear off both their faces.

"I thought we could all be together at home," Mike said again, subdued.

I can't remember how I responded or what I said to my kids, but I hope kindness won over irritation. I hope that, before I dialed into work to say I'd be late, I said I wished we could have a snow day, too. It was true. There was nothing I'd have liked more than to stay home with my kids, build snowmen, and drink hot chocolate. But it wasn't going to happen, so why even think about it? Reality was that I didn't get paid for days off and could hardly make ends meet. Still, I needed this job. It had medical benefits, something my last position had not offered. So, although my boss was the biggest jerk in the universe, I knew I was lucky to have the position.

The biggest jerk in the universe lectured me about my sloppy work ethic while I waited for the tea kettle to boil and my boys wilted in their too-warm clothes.

"I have to work late tonight to make up the time," I told Mike and Tim as I put down the phone and picked up the whistling kettle, along with car keys, purse, and Tim's backpack, which he was too small to carry. "By the time I finish working, it will be too dark to build a snowman. And you'll have to go to bed right after dinner, anyway." I said, biting off each bitter word as I marched them out to the car.

I hated the edge to my voice. Hated the woman divorce had turned me into—one with too little time for her children and zero patience for their lighthearted games. When had been the last time I'd felt light? How could I, now that working late meant paying the sitter overtime? Where would the money come from? I already lived so close to the bone that my income hovered at poverty level.

I knew this drab fact, because I'd looked into going back to college so I could get a better job, maybe as a teacher, matching my hours to those of my children. My income was so low that I qualified for a Pell grant: full tuition, books, and even liv- ing expenses. But I'd given up on the idea, just like I'd squashed snow day, because it wasn't practical. What would I do about insurance? And all the other costs that came with being a single parent? Plus, I was nearly thirty, too old to start college. What if I wasn't smart enough to finish a teaching program?

Before we even made it to the sitter's door, the snow began to fall again. It kept coming down all day. By noon, several new inches covered the ground. School let out early, but my sitter, who had children in the same classes as mine, took care of Mike and Tim.

At two o'clock, the county called a snow emergency, and a memo went out at the agency that everyone could leave early. My elation was short-lived, as my boss informed me that he needed me to stay late. The client wanted the new campaign ideas, and I had to type them.

I stayed and typed. What choice did I have? It had been my decision to divorce. I wanted a new life, a chance to live by my own rules. Now I had to make it work.

By the time I left the office, it was dark. It took forever to drive to the sitter's, and when I got there, Mike and Tim were sitting on her sofa watching television, while the sitter and her family sat in the next room eating family dinner. My heart split in half. Why hadn't she fed my boys?

"You're really late," was all she said.

The minute we got into the car, the tears I'd been holding back all day leaked out.

"Mommy, what's wrong?" Tim sounded scared. He was only four, after all.

I had to stop crying, be the grownup. If I needed to, I could cry later, when my sons were asleep. I quieted myself, sucking in deep breaths and blowing my nose. I decided to tell the truth, or part of it, anyway.

"I can't believe she didn't give you guys supper. Mommy's so sorry!" I backed the car out of the driveway.

As we made our way home through the snow, Mike told me how he made the hours go by until I picked them up. "You gave me Oreos for my snack, so before I ate one, I traced the pattern of the whole cookie on both sides. I thought by the time I traced all three cookies, you'd be there for sure."

Held-back tears scalding my throat, I stopped at the traffic light and glanced into the back seat at my brave boys. None of us voiced the obvious. I hadn't been there after the last Oreo. Guilt weighed me down like the thick inches of snow squatting on the roofs of houses we passed. Mike and Tim hadn't asked for any of this, and as bewildered as they often were by our changed circumstances, they rarely complained.

When we finally got back to the townhouse, I made macaroni and cheese. We sat eating the good, warm food in front of our window, watching the snow fly by the light of the security lamp that lit the parking lot.

After the boys were tucked into bed, stories had been read, and their eyes were closed in peaceful sleep, I didn't have a good cry like I'd planned. Instead, I pulled out the college information I'd filed away months ago. I had so many fears. Divorcing a man I no longer loved had been the last brave thing I'd done, or maybe it had been plain foolish. I flipped through the catalog, looking at the courses that had already begun, considering the chances I'd already missed. Would I be able to handle college-level courses? Would part-time work keep me and my children from worsened economic conditions? Would I find work as a teacher? None of it seemed possible. Yet, logically, I knew people succeeded at such things every day.

That night, as the snow filtered down on my world, I decided to do one more brave thing. After the snow stopped and the season changed to spring, I gathered my courage, quit my job, and went back to school. It was the bravest and best thing I've ever done, and it changed our three lives for the better.

My boys are grown men now, both college graduates with solid careers. A few years ago, Mike completed an advanced graduate degree. This past summer, Tim married a wonderful young woman. And me, I'm still teaching.

—Cynthia Harrison

The Long Thaw

I decided to spend New Year's Eve in a snow cave on the day my husband and I decided to get a divorce. It was also the week of the Clinton impeachment trials and the week the United States bombed Iraq; misery often loves company, yet the fact that other people were also having a bad day failed to comfort me.

I figured, rather than spend New Year's Eve home alone feeling sorry for myself, I'd go to the mountains, because mountains had always given me strength, and build myself a womb in the earth. Once the idea took hold, I couldn't let it go, partly because I anticipated being alone on New Year's anyway and partly because I couldn't resist the metaphor.

My last week with Jason, between Christmas and New Year's, is a blur of wet pillow cases, boxes of Kleenex, and deep-seated feelings of guilt and fear that made me sick to my stomach. Even water was hard to swallow. The only food I ate was a mistake: seafood gumbo. I can still taste the rancid sting of spices on an upset stomach. My body was rejecting everything.

I was twenty-two years old, too young to fully appreciate the responsibility of marriage but old enough to know that our rapidly diverging values would make it impossible for us to sustain a healthy relationship. I was determined to go to graduate school and travel around the world; Jason didn't see the point in leaving Montana. And the charming things I loved about Montana, the porch swings and huckleberry milkshakes, we never had.

The day before Jason left, I followed him around the house as we identified what would now belong to whom. The entire process was disgusting. I pretended it didn't bother me when he took half the bedroom set that I'd had since grade school and the furniture my parents had given us as a wedding present. We fought over CDs and photos, and when we started arguing about the bird feeder and wind chimes, I knew it was purely out of frustration and had little to do with what we thought we deserved. He got our dog, Klondike, and I got to feel a little less guilty by surrendering our most-loved possession.

Exhausted, Jason and I lay side by side and cried until tears would no longer come. At 5:00 A.M., after a sleepless night, I thought, *This is the last hour I will ever spend with you like this.*

I will always remember the last thing Jason did: Clutched by the sudden awareness that this parting was final, that things would never be the same, he grabbed me and sobbed, his chest heaving and the weight of his body pressing on my shoulders. "I can't imagine living without you," he said.

I wrapped my arms around his neck, my tears soaking his shirt sleeve.

"I was going to take you to Alaska next summer," he said. "What about the cabin in the mountains?"

"I know," I breathed, knowing he was well intended but that he would never follow through on it.

"I'm sorry I never built you a porch swing."

There was nothing more I could say.

The last time I saw Klondike, he was perched in the front seat of the Ryder truck, excited to go for a ride. His ears perked when he heard the engine, and he never looked back. As my husband, my dog, and half of my possessions headed south that New Year's Eve morning, I drove an hour west into the Bitterroot Mountains until the snow drifts were taller than my car. I stopped at a pullout along a Forest Service road, strapped on my snowshoes, adjusted my backpack, and headed up the hill. It would have been more convenient if New Year's was in July, but I couldn't wait for warm weather. January in Montana would have to do. Never mind that it was 26 degrees below zero.

The cold sucked the moisture from the snow. Snow drifts blew in dry, dusty swirls, and ice flakes collected in the folds of my Gore-Tex jacket. I kept looking back, to see where I'd come, to see if anything had moved, almost expecting someone to be there. Hiking was what Jason and I had in common, and when we were on a trail, it always seemed like we'd make it. He was as much a part of my wilderness experience as my boots were. Being without him now was like walking barefoot.

The snow wasn't as deep as I thought it would be, so I walked for a mile or so until I found what appeared to be a decent-sized drift. I was proud of my idea. How romantic to build a cave in the Bitterroot Mountains, to slough off the pain of the past year and emerge in a new one. I began to dig. As I dug, I would think about all the things I was angry at Jason for—his inability to turn down work for me, his resistance to change and travel, his dependency on alcohol. I would dig until the anger was gone. Until the pain of losing a friend was gone. Until the guilt of giving up on our marriage was gone. I would dig until my arms grew weak, until I couldn't strike the shovel into the snow one more time. Then sleep would come easily, and I would wait for the New

Year to begin so that I could be reborn and claim a fresh start. It would be that easy.

What actually happened was a little different. The skin on my face numbed and wrinkled. Snow ran across my shovel like sugar. I was not an experienced snow cave builder, and I couldn't hollow out a hole large enough for me to crawl into without collapsing the roof. After a while I began to think that I wasn't quite as clever as I had thought. The truth was that my plan boiled down to digging a hole and crawling into it.

It was getting dark on my cold, lonely hill. It would be a long night. I stopped digging and sat in my little snow pit out of the wind. For the first time in a long while, I felt alone. Even the mountains couldn't comfort me. I lay down on my side, burrowed in my sleeping bag, and rested my head on my backpack. Snow on the backpack felt rough against my cheek, like a man's unshaven face, and I cried for hours not knowing if I were missing Jason's face against mine or if I were relieved it was no longer there.

My cave looked more like a coffin than a womb, and after a few cold miserable hours, I packed up and headed back to the car.

What I didn't realize then was that breaking up with someone you once loved is a lifelong process that involves thousands of breakups. The initial separation is a tangible, tumultuous shearing. Other breakups happen, for example, five years later when you come across a Valentine's Day card he wrote, telling you that you are his entire world. That ache is deep but fleeting, especially if you have become strong enough and happy enough in your new life to transcend it.

What I also didn't realize on that cold, lonely hill was that digging holes in snow for the rest of my life would not erase pain from memory. Relief doesn't come from physical exertion or from communing with nature. It doesn't come from passing time or finding new love, either. It comes only in the blink of a moment when you know deep in your heart that what you've experienced in the past has helped you make a better decision today.

Those moments appear often these days, three years into a new marriage based on trust, love, and laughter. The terrible fights Jason and I had are but a memory of my past. When the littlest thing comes up, my husband and I address it immediately, and I try each day to be a loving, grateful partner. I doubt whether I could do that had I not first known what it was like to be an immature partner in an unsatisfy-ing marriage. These days, I am grateful for both my failed marriage and for my current, magical one.

—*Adrienne Lindholm*

Geronimo!

Being sixty-three years old yields varying responses in unexpected places, but even Victoria's Secret salesgirls manage to conceal their surprise when I shop there. Now, as a suddenly single, older female standing at the checkout counter of the Harpers Ferry Outfitters with flint, knife, and cup, I watched the young male cashier try to remain aloof, then start to speak . . . stop . . . and finally give in to curiosity.

"Are these a present for someone?" he asked, his eyes growing wide.

"No."

To his credit, he returned to task without betraying even a hint of amusement.

When I'd asked my son which items I should take on a solo camping trip, he said, "If you have a knife, a flint, and fifty feet of five-hundred-pound test rope, you can survive anywhere."

Well, maybe *he* can, since he'd successfully implemented a survival course in the mountains of Afghanistan, but I knew I would need considerably more than that short list. I purchased a Swiss Army knife and a flint. I didn't expect to use the flint, but I catapulted to outrageously "cool" in my own mind just by owning one.

For me, the truly essential purchase was the sixteen-ounce tin cup.

When I was nine or ten years old, my dad took our family on several outings we called "sleeping on the river." (We did not have a tent, and there was no official campground.) My sister and I would spend the day climbing and leaping from boulders while pretending to be Apache Indians allied with Geronimo in a life-and-death struggle for independence and autonomy. At night, we would sleep in the back of the pickup truck and search the skies for the Big Dipper. The next morning, I would bond with my father over bad coffee in a tin cup as we both squatted before the fire, squinting and spitting. Now, camping to me is all about that first cup of coffee by the early morning fire, sitting in silent contemplation, while flames, sun, and caffeine levels all rise at the same time.

The day of departure for my first solo camping adventure, the weather report promised unrelenting sunshine in the day, stars at night, and low humidity. Perfect. I drove into the Catoctin Mountains just as the weekend family campers drove out. Stopping at the camp store for firewood, I wondered aloud if I would be the only one on the grounds.

"No," said the clerk. "There are still a few others here, but the store is closing in an hour and won't open again until next weekend."

Before my separation from my husband, camping involved the men in my life: father, husband, or sons. They had built the fires, staked the tent, and in my mind at least, frightened away all "scary creatures." Now as I opened the new tent bag, I realized I should have tried to raise it at home first. But, what the heck, I could always sleep in the car if I had to. And after a half hour of struggling to get pole A to stay put in ring clip B while inserting pole C into ring clip D—failing and failing again—I believed I just might have to. *Can one person actually do this by herself?* I wondered. Thinking the car seats were sounding better all the time, I heaved a sigh of resignation and turned my thoughts to food preparation. Just then, the answer popped into my brain from nowhere: duct tape! A small piece would keep each pole in place just securely enough to raise the whole contraption, and I happened to have a roll in the car trunk. It worked! After tying the poles at the apex and tossing the sleeping bags inside, I zipped the door flap closed with a flourish and let out a squeal of triumph.

Next, the fire. Luckily, an Internet joke had circulated the week before: "How is it that a forest fire can start with only one match when it takes a whole box of matches to light a campfire?" The answer to the riddle is, of course, dead twigs and dry leaves; so, leaving nothing to chance, I had gathered a bag full of leaves and twigs on the hot, dry days before my trip. A half-box of matches was enough for my initiation with fire in the outdoors.

Roasted sausage, baked potato complete with sweet cream butter, bread, and water went down with the sun and the fire—each reflecting the other in red embers and in the glow from my contented body. Stars began to arrive slowly, like spaceships waiting for permission to land. An owl hooted a lullaby. With no clouds or rain forecast, I rejected the rain flap in favor of night sky and swaying treetops, slipped off my shoes, and zipped myself into the small tent. Whispering gratitude for the constancy of the Big Dipper, I then wished upon Sirius that I would live my life with enough independence and autonomy to choose occasional adventure over routine comfort, and fell asleep.

Footsteps disturbed me. *Probably someone going to the bath house*, I thought, and turned over, pulling the downy edges of the sleeping bag up a little higher. The footsteps came closer. I felt for my cell phone.

Why hadn't I programmed in the emergency number for camp security? Where was my whistle? Still in the car! I panicked as I heard the sound of my tent flap being unzipped. "Go away!" I struggled to yell. "You're at the wrong tent!" But nothing came out. My throat locked. I tried to scream.

Then I awoke from the nightmare.

I haven't felt so relieved since I was eight years old and the dentist announced "no cavities." But next time, I resolved, I will bring my whistle into the tent and program my cell phone with the security number.

In the morning, deep whiffs of frying bacon intoxicated me as I squatted by the fire sipping bitter coffee and watching the flames mingle with the rising sun. Soon a vision formed. Was it really in the smoke or just in my head? No matter. I clearly "saw" a road/camping trip to Wyoming.

Later, while driving down the mountain, I remembered something I had read: "When you are falling, dive." I had not understood the words then, but suddenly I got it. Growing older brings inevitable solitude. Husbands leave, parents and friends die, children marry and move away. One way to "dive" is to embrace the increasing time alone with absorbing adventures that only you can do. That, I think, is a leap I can make.

—*S. Ann Robinson*

That Magic Moment

Friends help us move our belongings to our new apartment first thing that Saturday morning. I remain behind to clean, solemnly, the half-empty house during the afternoon. My husband arrives home just as I finish. For whatever reason, I need to leave the house clean for him. The cleaning is my last goodwill gesture.

As I walk out the door, looking back to say goodbye, his caustic words hit hard one more time, "You'll never make it on your own."

I silently close the door. I turn away from the house of my dreams and my husband of seventeen years and never look back. It took me years to get the courage to take this step. Now, here I am, walking away from solid monetary security and the man I'd planned to grow old with.

My daughters hug me warmly as I arrive at our new home that evening. The apartment, though very old and dark, provides a haven of calm for us. We begin from here. With friction removed from our daily lives, we soon begin to flourish.

So many details change immediately. It's all about succeeding. The new job I found right before I left my husband proves to be exciting. My boss and coworkers relate well to my perfectionism in my daily tasks and also to the strong common sense I bring to the mix. I quickly succeed in all avenues of managing a distribution center office. Everything fascinates me: bills of lading, the nuances for loading a tractor trailer, receiving bulk products to break down for distribution, and much more. As these daily work tasks blend into my daily hectic schedule with my teenage daughters, my husband's last words to me keep ringing in my ears, "You'll never make it on your own."

I work hard to build a nice home for us. At first, it is difficult, as I don't make much money. Having good insurance, though, provides peace of mind through some major issues for my daughters, one with cancer and one with psychological issues. After a year's time, I get a raise. Although it's not much extra money, it provides me with the satisfaction that I can progress in my job successfully.

I am driven to succeed, understanding that my earnings are the basis for paying for everything in our lives. My eldest daughter helps with a part-time job after school and weekends, but it is still not enough, even though she pays for her car insurance and gasoline. Soon I begin using credit cards to pay for incidentals, medicine, and unexpected expenses. The added debt now looms overhead like a dark cloud, always following me.

After a few years of working at my job, I receive several raises and several Employee-of-the-Month awards. My work style makes its way to the attention of the president of my company. With no warning at all, I receive a promotion, a big raise, and the request for me to move to our home office customer support team in the Midwest. The opportunity is too great to pass up, and quite abruptly, I say goodbye to my grown daughters and find myself in Michigan, beginning the next step of a career. I never thought too much about a "career" before, but now the word is appropriate.

I thrive in the new environment. After several discussions with the company's president, I am confident that what I bring to the table is giving a fresh outlook to the customer service center. Again, I am blessed with huge successes at work, eventually being promoted to the team's manager. With this promotion and raise, I'm finally able to pay off the old credit card bills that grew so quickly when I first left my husband.

On the office bulletin board one morning I see a posting of an opportunity for training and using a specific computer application with a new customer support division being created in Connecticut, where the corporate offices are located. I apply, get the position, and again do well with another endeavor. Work is my solace for any loneliness I feel and my substitute for many personal areas of my life. I tell myself that once I succeed, everything will be the way I want it to be in my life. I'll prove my ex-husband's words to be false. Somehow, his words are always in my mind.

Although my career blossoms, I have a yearning to learn more about the new computer application I learned during my last job change. One thing concerns me, though: My resume includes no information about a college background. I never attended college.

I beef up my resume, including everything I know about working with the computer application. It sounds good to me. I pray that a company out there will want me as much as I want to move ahead. Too bad, I think, that there isn't an appropriate place on a resume for "common sense" or "good business sense." That could offset the fact that I don't have college information on my resume. This inner demon follows me. I regularly fight it, and yet, I know I will succeed as long as I use logic and perseverance.

Listening to coworkers and hearing about the need of consulting companies for people like me provides me with knowledge on how to sell myself. My new job search takes me about two months, resulting in multiple interviews at different consulting companies and two job offers. Accepting one of the offers places me into the brave new world of consulting for the computer application I learned and involves considerable traveling. Creative negotiating on my part increases my salary by 50 percent. I am on top of the world. I move forward immediately, being assigned to a client in Indianapolis. A new life for me begins again.

My ex-husband goes on with his life, too. He struggles terribly with his health, his job, and his relationships with his daughters. Eventually, he remarries. After only a few years, his second marriage ends traumatically and he loses his job of twenty years. I am always aware of his struggles, since I remain close to his sister and his mother and since my daughters, too, mention parts of what happens to him.

Working at a client site in Pasadena, California, my career is at its ultimate high. My eldest daughter lives close by the client site. Even though we're both busy working, I enjoy the opportunity to see her regularly whenever the chance arises. She calls me one morning to ask me a favor for her dad. She explains that he needs to get to the airport and asked her for a ride. Since she knows I am going home to Georgia the same day and close to the same time, would I please pick him up and take him to the airport with me so she won't miss work? At first, I don't want to, but then think better of it as my daughter explains what bad shape he is in. He's traveling to Connecticut to spend time with his sister.

Driving to the airport, our conversation is pleasant, and he explains the details of his damaged life. Even after the heartache I experienced with him for seventeen years, pity is all I can feel for him. Ironically, we travel with the same airlines and our gates are right next to each other. We both check in and sit together to wait for our flights.

As my flight begins to board, there is an announcement for me to come to the desk at the gate. It takes me only a minute for the airline to upgrade me to first class. It's an upbeat moment for me, as the cross-country flight is long and first class makes it more comfortable.

I hug my ex-husband goodbye and turn away to go. With pride in his voice he says, "You really made it on your own, didn't you?" I smile as I walk away.

—Amy E. Zajac

A Potato Epiphany

There I stood, hoe in hand in the hot sun, resting a back that was complaining about bending over the seemingly unending rows of Pontiac potatoes that needed to be hilled up and weeded. It was a gorgeous day with lazy puffs of white moving across a brilliant, clear-blue sky.

That year, the patch of 1,500 hills was planted on the east side of "the acreage," across the main road from the McBride Reservoir. The acreage was the hub of our family's life—business office and home for my husband's parents, where they gardened for the pleasure of it. We lived in town in their old home, built by my husband's father and grandfather.

As I checked the developing blisters on my palms, I watched the trailered sailboats and power-boats hurrying by so their owners could enjoy the beautiful summer day on the man-made haven of

McBride. *Must be nice to be able to afford the boat and the time for such an enticing activity,* I thought.

All of our family's summer weekends were spent either picking peas, pulling radishes, culling strawberries, or harvesting raspberries. At least with those chores, you could enjoy eating some of the crop, helping you forget the aching back or knees. We were there to please my husband's father and his wants, without regard to ours.

Looking over the innocent potato plants at my feet, rebellious thoughts formed. After eleven years of marriage and no vacations, not even a honeymoon, I was beginning to mutiny. To be fair, it was difficult for my husband to get away when he was the only employee working with his parents in their delivery business. But that shouldn't mean all of us, even the kids, had to sacrifice our weekends to follow my father-in-law's dictates—especially since there were no thanks. Of course, there was all the fresh produce we could eat, but that hardly made up for a life with no leisure activities.

My father-in-law grew up on a farm and was reliving his youth at the expense of ours. Driving the tractor, operating the potato digger or corn planter, he was a happy man. In fact, I could hear the chuff-chuff of the red Pony as he cultivated the corn on the other side of the corncrib. On a Sunday ten years earlier and six weeks before my due date, I was driving that Pony down this very field while my husband pitched manure off the wagon that trailed behind. Four hours later, I held my first baby in my arms, small but healthy. Thinking about it made me realize the price we could have paid for being unpaid truck farmers.

The only thing that made my father-in-law happier than riding the Pony was taking bags of potatoes, tomatoes, sweet corn, or whatever was in season on his route. He loved the compliments and thanks he got as he gave them away while explaining that Pontiacs were the best all-round potato cultivated.

Wonder how many potatoes we use in a year for our family of four? I thought to myself, watching yet another flotilla of boats pass on the road. *The kids, at eight and ten, don't eat much food at all. I'll bet we eat less than five pounds a week. Five times fifty-two weeks and that's roughly two-hundred-fifty pounds a year.*

I looked across at my husband attacking a particularly large weed in his row, sweat dripping off his chin. "How much do potatoes cost in the store?"

He glanced at me with a puzzled look on his face.

"I don't know. I don't do any of the shopping." Because I wasn't a whiner or nagger, he had no idea how I felt or what I was thinking.

"Well, I never buy potatoes, so I don't know either." But I could guess.

To myself again: *Let's use twenty cents a pound, times two-hundred-fifty pounds; that's up to fifty dollars a year. Now, how long does it take me to earn fifty dollars as a college teacher?* Okay, $10,800 for nine months would be $1,200 a month, approximately twenty working days to a month, which would be $60 a day. In less than one day of teaching, I could pay for all the potatoes we eat in a whole year. I'm sure store-boughts would be fine. *And I sure enjoy teaching much more than baking in the sun while giving up another weekend,* I said to myself, glaring at the offending plants.

The frustration made the hoe dig deeper and faster into the weeds.

Later, back at home, nobody seemed to notice that in the kitchen, pans were banging and cupboard doors were slamming a little more loudly than usual.

The next day at the store, I checked. Indeed, a pound of potatoes cost twenty cents.

That night at the dinner table, I said to my husband, "Do you know how much it would cost us for a year's potatoes if we were buying them at the store?"

He stopped the fork halfway to his mouth. "No," he said, with a look that said, "and who cares, when we grow our own?"

"Well, I figured it out yesterday, and I earn enough teaching in just one day to cover the year."

I expected to hear a rerun of his dad's lecture about how much better the Pontiacs were and that you couldn't get them in the store, although the Kennebec potatoes, like our neighbor grew, were almost as good. Instead, he merely shrugged his shoulders and went back to eating. He wasn't a whiner or nagger, so I didn't know what he was thinking, either.

The next night when he returned from his job and working at the acreage, as usual, he handed me a ten-dollar bill.

"What's this for?" I asked.

"My dad sent it for your day's work in the patch."

I was so upset and insulted I couldn't say a thing. He had tattled to his dad, and I was certain he hadn't defended me against whatever his dad had said. He'd just acted as a messenger boy. Just then, I had an epiphany that helped me to take the step that was the beginning of my self-esteem and led to the end of the marriage. I took the ten bucks without saying a word and never hoed another potato again.

—*Faye "Sunny" Glessner*

First You Cry

We entered two at a time, reminding me of beasts climbing aboard Noah's ark. But, instead of twosomes floating on the sea together, we were all sinking in the stormy ocean of divorce. Some were solemn and wordless as they waited for the judge. Others angrily whispered at each other. I walked beside Mark, my soon-to-be former husband, as we entered the courtroom, where we, along with all these other couples, sought no-fault divorces. Of course, the term, no-fault, was a euphemism for "it's both our faults."

I was numb, having spent my tears the previous days and nights. All that remained today were the puffy eyes, the reddened nose, and the dull headache that accompanied too much distress and too little sleep.

Each couple had a number giving the order in which they would appear before the judge. We were number twenty-two, one of the last. As the other twosomes marched up to the judge, I sat in a sort of trance, folding and refolding our ticket number until I mangled it so much it was almost unreadable.

After a while, as couple after couple was announced free and unencumbered, it actually became entertaining in a macabre way. Imagining what brought them to this point took my mind off my own miserable situation. I figured the fourteenth couple to be in their seventies, both well-dressed and attractive. Thirty-five years of marriage was dissolved in four minutes. Afterward, though, I discovered the reason. The man had a gorgeous younger woman waiting for him. The woman had an almost-pretty young man doing the same.

Finally, it was our turn. When I stood, my stomach was still on the bench and my mouth felt raw from chewing the inside of my cheek. The ticket, now in tatters, fluttered off my lap.

Inside my head, a little voice judged me much harsher than the man wearing the robe would: *I couldn't make it work. I'm such a loser.* The voice grew louder with each step I took toward the judge, until I thought it would drown out what he was saying. Mark nudged me.

"I'm sorry, sir. Could you repeat what you said?" I timidly asked.

"Are you in agreement with the dissolution of this marriage?" the judge barked impatiently.

"Yes, I am," my voice cracked.

It was over. We walked out of the courtroom, suddenly uncomfortable with each other.

Mark looked down and mumbled, "It wasn't that bad, was it?" as if I had just had elective surgery.

Staring at my feet, all I could manage was, "At least it's over."

He sighed with relief. "And it's no reflection on either of us. We just made a mistake. We handled it like adults, and now we can get on with our lives."

He was trying to absolve himself. To do that, he had to include me in the absolution. But I was hurt and resented being alone in the pain. I wanted to scream, "I don't feel like an adult. I feel like a kid whose dream has been spoiled." Tears of frustration threatened to pour out, and accusing words ached to spew from my mouth. I turned and tramped away.

I was shaking as I drove. How could I get on with my life? My life had been a married one, not perfect, but one I mostly enjoyed. To my surprise, though, the enjoyment hadn't been mutual. I didn't know that, of course, until Mark had betrayed me six months prior to our appearance at court.

I arrived at my mother's house. After I'd forbidden her or anyone to come with me to court, she had made me promise to visit right afterward. Wordlessly, she opened the door and held out her arms as she had so many times before, trying to heal the bruises her daughter received as she navigated through her bumpy life. I tried not to cry, but as soon as I felt her warmth, I knew it was hopeless. The tears stung my already raw cheeks.

"Honey." My mother's sympathetic tears wet my hair. "I know it hurts really badly right now, but you'll come out of it."

My continuing tears told her I doubted that.

After a short silence, she released me and went to the refrigerator. She pulled out a Diet Pepsi and then, from the cupboard, homemade double-chocolate muffins. My mother knew the value of comfort food. She set them down and sat next to me as I swallowed a big gulp of the soda. I picked up a muffin, and its chocolate mushiness soothed my hurt feelings for a blessed moment.

Mom watched me carefully. "Stay here tonight."

I nodded as my throat closed again and even the silky chocolate couldn't flow through.

I slept through the night, but felt exhausted the next morning. As the disorientation of sleep disappeared, I remembered the day before. A heavy, black feeling came over me. I was terrified that if I didn't move immediately it would immobilize me, so I threw off the covers and headed to the bathroom.

By the time I returned to my mother's kitchen, my eyes were red again. With my head down I silently slid into a chair at the table. Without a word, she moved to cradle my head against her breast. "It's over, Carole. Cry when you need to, but get yourself ready to move on. It's not easy, but you don't have a choice."

I started to protest that she didn't understand, until I remembered her own grief when my father died seven years before. He had been her husband for twenty-nine years.

We talked that morning. About losing a dream and how waking up without that dream makes you feel naked, vulnerable, and angry.

Morning turned into afternoon, and my stomach's growling was drowning out our conversation. "Mom, let's go to lunch. I'm hungry."

She looked startled but quickly agreed. Over lunch and in the following days we became good friends. Over time, ours grew to be a relationship I reveled in. When I was a teen, I didn't think my mom understood me. When I became a young married woman, I never had enough time to spend with her.

Now, she revealed her struggles during those early days after my father died. I learned about her decision to enjoy life again—and that every morning when she woke up, she made that decision again. I finally understood from this four foot, ten inch woman what it was to be strong and independent. How to move on, no matter what.

Three years later, Mom's generous heart gave out and she died. I grieved fiercely for two years and continue to miss her love and friendship. But I also remember her wise and caring words: "Cry when you need to, but get yourself ready to move on." Those words live in my heart still, there whenever I need them. Today, I think not about whatever unhappy situation I might find myself in, but rather about the kind, loving woman who, along with a hug, gave me a living example of her own wisdom. With a silent thanks to Mom, I follow her lead.

—*Carole Fowkes*

We Meet Again

I didn't know who he was, but something about him seemed familiar—like meeting someone for the first time, only you feel like you've met him before, in some other lifetime, maybe, or some other universe. Certainly my universe had recently collapsed. After almost eleven years of marriage, my husband had declared he was leaving, and a few minutes later he did exactly that with a final slam of the door to cover the sound of my scream and sudden collapse to the floor.

Okay, that was a bit melodramatic. He didn't actually slam the door, it just felt like it. But my collapsing like a puppet with its strings cut, that much is real. And I know I made some sort of anguished cry, because weeks later he told me he'd heard it, had hurt to hear it, but not enough to turn back. That was about five months ago.

When people ask, I tell them he went in search of his dreams, beyond the confinement of love and marriage. I don't say that one of his dreams was another woman. That's an admission that cuts too deep, and besides, I don't need the "I'm so sorry" looks from friends and family. I need their expressions to say, "We're here for you"—and oh, how I love them for that.

So, anyway, about this strangely familiar guy—the first thing I noticed was his smile, perhaps because he was smiling at me as I walked into the training room. Though I didn't recognize him, I returned the grin by polite habit, figuring his happiness was relief that I had arrived. I'm a sign language interpreter, and once I'm on the scene, all the hearing folks breathe a little easier; no more tedious notes passed back and forth to communicate with the deaf employee.

Smiling Guy introduced himself to the group; my hands followed his words, including his name, which I finger-spelled, but I still couldn't place him. I was used to people recognizing me at work while I drew a blank regarding them. I'm the only sign language interpreter for our dozen hearing-impaired employees, and the job keeps me up front most of the time, easy to spot.

Still, there was something about this guy that was like a wisp of a warm memory. And something else: a growing, glowing tingle. What was that about?

Probably he had taken the sign language class I teach onsite, or perhaps he was a manager I had chatted with in some obscure hallway. Whoever he was, his ready smile was a sweet drink, indeed.

He finished his opener and stepped aside for the second presenter to take his turn. That's when the coughing fit hit me. It started as a tickle in my throat but progressed into full-on coughing, the kind that refused to be ignored. I stopped the instructor for "just a minute" and began to rise, but suddenly he was there, kneeling down with a Styrofoam cup of water. I took it, surprised but grateful.

"Thank you," I said when able.

He stood up. "You are most welcome."

Wow.

The lecture began again and so did my hands, but my mind was distracted by the puzzle: Where had we met before?

He sought me out during break and asked about my upcoming signing class. "Is there still room?" he asked.

"Certainly," I said, smiling too much.

Then he was gone, retreating to prepare for his turn in front of the class. Something stirred in me, barely noticeable, but for a timeless second . . . I had missed him.

I became alarmed—and intrigued. As I continued interpreting, I kept stealing glances and wondering where we had encountered each other before and how I could possibly remember a stranger so fondly. Then during lunch I was both pleased and nervous when he appeared at my table in the cafeteria.

"Hi. Mind if join you?"

There's that smile, again. I know that smile. "No, fine, go ahead."

I studied my salad as though I had forgotten what I had just placed on my plate, but any contrived calm didn't last long as he settled in across from me. I felt so awake in his easy presence; pleasurable feelings suddenly released from their pain-imposed dormancy.

I attempted a ration of inward control, trying to make sense of this reaction, so quick and strong. I assured myself that everything was as normal as it had been prior to my arrival that morning. He was sitting here with me because he wanted to know more about the sign-language class, or maybe he wanted to learn how to sign something beforehand. Yes, that was it. Some tangible reason, please, that I can understand and name.

He cleared his throat. "So what do you like to do? What kind of music do you listen to?"

I looked up. He was curious about me? I looked closer. He seemed sincere.

"Jazz," I lied. It sounded so much better than my real inclination toward the top ten pop tunes and watered-down rock and roll. But he accepted it; my credibility unchallenged and assured.

The conversation continued—and continued to engage me. I would have been content merely to be included in the discussion, and I was more than happy to be the center of it, instead. He wanted to know what I thought, how I reasoned—and why did I like baseball so much? After a while, I stopped worrying about how I knew him and just enjoyed the feelings his coaxing inquiries invoked. At times, he would casually disclose some of his thoughts and life's interests to me. That was just as thrilling.

What he didn't know was how wonderful it was to see him again. Because I knew by the hour's end that my memory had not deceived me. This was no stranger sharing my table, my space, but a cherished, long-lost friend from my past, before I was married, before my husband had left me.

It had just been so long since I'd seen him that I'd almost forgotten the pleasure of his company. But in his steady gaze, I remembered. He was Mr. Interested.

—*Barbara Neal Varma*

What I Know Now

After my year of battling cancer with chemotherapy, radiation, no hair, and no strength, my husband of twenty-five years walked into our bedroom and told me his needs had not been met for a long time and he had met someone else. He wanted a separation. I thought he was kidding at first.

I was a stay-at-home mom of five children. The two oldest were in college, but the youngest was only four. So I did what any woman in that situation would do: I panicked. I begged him to stay and work things out. And he did stay, physically. I ran to counselors, preachers, doctors, you name it. I did everything I could think of to save our marriage, except the one thing he said he wanted: I didn't conquer my weight problem. After five years of trying to fix our marriage alone, I finally gave up and filed for divorce. He simply didn't love me.

What I have learned from my divorce could fill all the pages in the Library of Congress. One of my biggest lessons has been that of patience. Patience with myself, to allow my healing to take place. Patience with my children as they learned the new dynamics of our family. Patience with friends and family who didn't understand why I couldn't just "move on" and "get over it" faster.

Each person's divorce is unique, so the issues differ. But here are some of the things that I have learned from my divorce:

- I learned that no matter how many shirts you ironed, clothes you washed, and meals you prepared during thirty years of marriage, it counts for nothing with some men—and it counts for little with some courts.
- I learned that security is an illusion.
- I learned that what I suspected about my husband's late nights and business trips over those thirty years was, in fact, true.
- I learned that all the religion and respectability in the world count for nothing if your husband thinks another woman is more exciting than you are.
- I learned that there are a lot of books on divorce and forgiveness.

- I learned that there are a lot of worthless books.
- I learned that you can't make someone love you, and if you try to force love, you become a manipulative nightmare of a person you no longer recognize—and then it is difficult to love yourself.
- I learned the value of the Psalms.
- I learned to wait on God's plan.
- I learned that my children help me to keep my routine, and that keeps the depression at bay.
- I learned that not all kids need therapy because of divorce, but that seeing a therapist to make sure they're okay is a good idea.
- I learned that my children and I laugh more and are more ourselves now.
- I learned that children are smart and that their love and respect can't be bought with money or things.
- I learned that no matter how hard I try to be positive and hopeful, sometimes it is better to stay in bed.
- I learned to let go of the bitterness, so everyone doesn't run when my divorce and I walk into a room.
- I learned to stop talking about the divorce long before the bitterness was gone.

- I learned—when it comes to custody and visitation—to do what is in the kids' best interests, even when it's not what you want to do.
- I learned—when it comes to money—to settle for no less than what five children and thirty years of my life are worth.
- I learned that giving up your education for his is just plain stupid.
- I learned that it is okay to be older than your professors.
- I learned that outside appearance is very important in some relationships.
- I learned that I am not interested in that kind of relationship.
- I learned that I am beautiful, talented, and self-disciplined.
- I learned that you don't have to be friends with your ex-husband.
- I learned that sending his clothes flying off the second-floor balcony into the dirt is therapeutic.
- I learned that the pain of cancer pales in comparison to the pain of divorce.
- I learned never to make any permanent decisions when you are in such pain. I learned that, when the pain is gone, you won't care, and that is the ultimate revenge.

- I learned that some days nothing satisfies me like planning my revenge. But then I remember, "Revenge is a dish best served cold."
- I learned that keeping a journal helps you to work through the ever-changing emotions of divorce with dignity and without subjecting your children to your pain or overburdening your family and friends with your angst.
- I learned not to send emotionally charged, divorce-related e-mails until twenty-four hours after I've written them. Things almost always look better after a good night's sleep.
- I learned that you don't have to like your lawyer; she just has to be good.
- I learned that arguing about the dining room chandelier makes the judge laugh.
- I learned that there are professionals to call for broken-down cars.
- I learned that cobwebs can be nature experiments.
- I learned that frozen waffles are fine for dinner every now and again.
- I learned that a messy house doesn't make me a failure.
- I learned that all failure can be learned from.
- I learned that the last thing to return is your sense of humor.

- I learned that laughing at your ex-husband until you wet yourself might not be nice, but it is great therapy.
- I learned the joy and freedom that come from getting out from under the influence of someone's judgment.
- I learned how to run a 200-acre farm.
- I learned that I like football.
- I learned that I can turn my music up loud and sing.
- I learned that leaving an unhappy marriage can make you wiser, smarter, more secure, and a lot more fun to be with.
- I learned there is no limit to the possibilities my future holds. Even though I am fifty, I have a lot left to offer this world and I am excited about it.
- I learned that there comes a point in time when it has all been said.
- When I reached that point, I learned that forgiveness is for my healing, not to purge his guilt.

Finally, I learned that you don't have to mend fences to forgive; you can just walk away.

—*Jane Ann Hiteshew Holland*

Thief of Hearts

"Mommy, did somebody steal our house?" my four-year-old daughter, Piper, asked as we backed from the driveway of our beautiful home for the last time.

Somebody had stolen our house—and the thief was named Dee Vorce. I didn't have the heart to tell Piper that half of everything we owned, our friendly neighbors, our sense of stability, and our family income had gone missing as well. If lucky, the children wouldn't recognize my panic when I plucked bills from the mailbox, received my medical insurance premium, and interviewed for a job for the first time in six years. Instead of telling Piper our dreadful future, I smiled and planned to call up the "home is where you make it" speech along with the "it will be an adventure" mantra that I had practiced for weeks. Unfortunately, the words lodged in my throat below the "goodbye" I had intended for my old life on our way out the door.

The children and I pulled up to our so-called "luxury" apartment that allowed for our dog, and I thanked God we didn't have to cut loose the family pet along with everything else we had forfeited. Walking into the place transported me back to my college days, and I pictured us eating ramen noodles and hot dogs for dinner each night. *We'd get used to this*, I thought.

My son, Holden, raced around, pointing out all the amenities, as if on vacation. Little did the kids know, this vacation would last longer than a week or two. With sole responsibility for rent, electric, car insurance, medical bills, garbage collection fees, cable, and groceries, I would have to conserve the money I had squirreled away from the sale of the house, needing it to stretch until I could find employment. I did a decent job of penny-pinching, until the children boasted about their father's elegant house on the newest golf course in town, their weekends with him that rivaled a trip to Disney World, and the high-tech gadgets he bought them.

"We can't afford—" I started, but then quickly switched gears, "—to miss the big sale at Toys "R" Us." Off we went on a guilt-reduction excursion.

As Holden and Piper stocked the cart with their fondest wishes, I rationalized that the children loved both ramen noodles and hot dogs. Seven hundred dollars later, toys littered the living room floor, and a temporary sense of pride washed over me, even though Piper's new Barbie Talking Townhouse appeared half the size of our apartment. My former privileged life taunted me as my daughter arranged the posh furnishings in Barbie's elaborate dwelling. I secretly bemoaned that Piper had to decorate the place—that even Barbie couldn't afford a professional designer on a single woman's salary.

That night, as I studied the receipt from our impromptu purchases, I recognized my pathetic attempt to buy my children's forgiveness for leaving their father and ruining their lives. I felt small enough to climb into Barbie's splendid home, yet unworthy of surrounding myself with such beauty.

Guilt had stolen my good judgment in more ways than one. I decided to remain a stay-at-home mom even though my expenses nibbled at my savings. The thought of placing Piper in day care and sending Holden to after-school care was less than appealing. My children's crazy pleas to eat chocolate ice cream while sitting on the cream-colored sofa and to watch one more cartoon before bedtime were met with a resounding "yes." How could I deny them such rewards when forcing them to shuttle between two houses?

So, when the man in the upstairs apartment asked me out on a date, I met his request with a resounding "yes." The date would be my reward for managing to get through yet another day, stowed away in that tiny apartment.

The following Saturday, while the children spent the night at their father's, I nervously checked my lipstick, my hair, and my dress several times while waiting for Michael to knock on the door. *Surely he likes the color red,* I thought. *Doesn't every man?* When he arrived, looking more handsome than I remembered, my breath caught and I realized how long it had been since anyone had elicited such a response.

Over dinner, Michael and I discovered common bonds: children, dogs, a passion for writing, and painful divorces. As we talked and laughed, there were moments that I struggled to catch my breath. *Just nerves,* I told myself, and attempted to finish my dinner. Then my heart began to race, and I grimaced as my hand instinctively clutched my chest.

"Are you okay?" Michael asked, noticing my discomfort.

"Sure," I lied, flushing with embarrassment.

"Do we need to go?"

Was it that noticeable? I wondered. "Oh God, no. I'll be fine," I said, trying to convince myself as much as Michael.

The physical duress soon exhausted me; I felt as though I had run a marathon. Once home, Michael walked me to my apartment door. I blurted good night, closed the door, and went straight to bed. For a few moments, I lay quietly, reflecting upon our lovely evening and the possibility of seeing him again, until the overwhelming pounding in my chest drowned out the pleasant thoughts.

Over the next several weeks, Michael and I shared dinners, lunches, and nightly phone calls. At times my heart beat so fast I could no longer hold a conversation, and I'd end our talk early out of fear of passing out mid-sentence. A hopeless romantic, I wanted to think my heart was making up for lost time or that it was sending me a sign that Michael was the man for me. One evening, when my heart raced for more than an hour, I went to the hospital. The emergency room doctor soon informed me the problem was physiological. It had nothing to do with my newfound love. During my consultation with the cardiologist, he confirmed this notion when he handed me a heart monitor to wear for two weeks. His suspicion: *supraventricular tachycardia.*

"Supra what?" I gazed at the monitor, picturing a hand-knitted shawl draped over my shoulders and a cane in my right hand.

I didn't feel much better when the cardiologist explained that abnormal electrical connections were overriding my heart's natural pacemaker, causing my heart to beat uncontrollably.

You've got to be kidding me, I thought, as I drove home from the physician's office. I stared at the equipment that would nuzzle up to my intimate body parts. Michael and I had movie tickets for the evening. How would I hide such a monstrosity while on a romantic date?

Luckily for me, it was turtleneck season, and I had plenty of oversized sweaters and jackets. As long as the monitor didn't beep and Michael didn't have a sudden urge to embrace me, I figured I'd be fine.

Unfortunately, my covert plan failed when the need for dumpster-diving arose.

"Are you sure you threw out the monitor?" Michael called from inside the metal dumpster at our apartment complex, his voice rattling much like my heart.

"Yes," I said, panicked about replacing the high-priced equipment. "At least, I think so."

After searching through the garbage for nearly two hours, we called it a loss. Later that night, we found the monitor inside my apartment.

"I'm so sorry," I offered. "I truly thought I'd lost it."

Michael hadn't found anything of value in that big, smelly bin. But I had found a man who picked through a hundred people's garbage to help me—a man who apparently was not scared off by my defective heart.

The monitor's recordings and other tests revealed the need for heart surgery. Only thirty-nine, I had never thought to prepare myself for such a possibility.

The day of my surgery, Michael clasped my hand as I lay on the gurney. My face held not an ounce of make-up, and the stylish cap covering my hair resembled the one my grandmother hung on her showerhead. Yet, the concern in Michael's eyes clearly told of his feelings for me, whether I appeared attractive or not.

"I'll be here when you're out of surgery." Then he bent down and whispered, "I love you."

"I love you, too," I choked out, holding back tears.

As they wheeled me to the operating room, images of my children's innocent faces and thoughts of mounting medical bills, my prolonged unemployment, and the possibility of my death swirled around in my head. *Please God, nothing bad can happen now,* I prayed. *Not after waiting this long to find a man like Michael.* The nurse plastered a tangle of electrodes to my chest. After seven hours of surgery, the doctor proclaimed the procedure a success. My heart would now beat in a normal rhythm, and within a few months my physical endurance would return to normal.

Michael stood at my bedside. "You know, you're high maintenance," he joked, as he stroked my cheek. "But I like it."

"Yeah, I'm a little surprised you didn't bolt after the dumpster-diving incident."

"What, and miss all this excitement?"

Later, as dusk fell and sleepiness began to overtake me, Michael tucked the blanket underneath my chin, brushed my hair back from my face, and leaned over and kissed me.

"Goodnight, sweetheart. I'll call you tomorrow morning," I said.

"I'm not going anywhere," he said, pointing to the chair next to the bed.

As Michael watched over me that night, I swear my heart fluttered once again.

As we pulled from the parking lot of the apartment complex with the last of our belongings in tow, Piper said, "Mommy, I think somebody stole our apartment."

"Yes, honey," I said with a smile, catching a glimpse of my handsome new husband in the rearview mirror, following us to our new home. "They most certainly did."

This time, my children and I rejoiced that there was another thief—the kind and loving man who had stolen our hearts.

—*Cathi LaMarche*

I'll Take the High Road

After today I will finally be divorced, for real—finally! I smile to myself as I drive the seven miles to the Dukes County courthouse. I didn't sleep well last night, but after taking a hot shower this morning and gobbling down a stack of pancakes, I am now feeling fine. I bounce to the beat of the music blasting from my stereo and take another sip of coffee. As I brush my bangs away from my face, I notice a man hitchhiking at the side of the road. He waves, and I recognize him. He is my soon-to-be ex-husband. *Should I stop and give him a ride . . . or not?*

I need to make the decision quickly, leaving no time to replay the last three years leading to this moment. If time allowed, the film would begin on the day I left the courthouse with temporary divorce orders.

"We cannot finalize the divorce yet," my attorney explained, "because your husband is demanding that you sell your jointly owned house and split the funds with him. That would leave you and your four children on the streets."

Although I was thrilled that the temporary orders allowed me to remain in the family home with my children, the responsibilities loomed before me. It also meant I would be living in a limbo existence of not really being divorced but not really being married either.

My husband, his trim blonde hair and face bronzed from sun and surfing, walked out of the courtroom on the arm of his new girlfriend to celebrate. Because he owned a successful painting business and had moved into his girlfriend's house, he was set for an easy transition and a comfortable future. He wouldn't have to worry about child care schedules or stretching a meager budget.

"You'll never make it without me," he snickered, "You won't be able to take care of everything."

During the first few days following the court hearing for the legal separation, in between weeping and praying, I scrambled to improve my finances. I rented a spare bedroom to my friend, Bill, a plumber in need of temporary housing. I increased my hours at work, juggling my schedule so that I would still be available to my children.

One day my ex-husband and some of his buddies cruised by me in a Jeep with the top down. The sun shone on their windblown hair as they smoked cigarettes and laughed. They didn't notice me walking up the hill from the post office, carrying a letter from the bank warning that our house was going into foreclosure. Apparently, my husband had not been paying our household bills for months before he left.

"You'll never be able to make it alone," his taunts echoed in my mind as I trudged on.

When I got home, I made a series of phone calls. Cradling the phone on my shoulder, I chopped, stirred, and poured, creating a casserole for my children to eat, while I ranted and cried to my sister, then my mom, and then a few friends.

Feeling a bit better after having let off some steam, I began to look for avenues of help. It took a few days, but after following a trail of telephone numbers for community help centers, I tracked down an agency that agreed to pay my past-due mortgage. My house was out of foreclosure.

A few days later, I noticed a man from the Tis-bury Water Department standing in my yard. Realizing I was staring at him with a puzzled look on my face, he motioned for me to open the window.

"I've been sent to shut off your water," he explained, his face full of compassion.

"Oh . . . " was the only reply I could muster.

"Look," the kind man suggested, "why don't you see if you can come up with the past-due amount this morning, and go to the office and pay it. I'll do my other calls and come back to your house as my last stop."

After withdrawing some funds from my skimpy savings account, I rushed down to pay the bill. The water continued to flow from my faucets.

Later that summer, I stepped into the shower and—yikes! Icy cold water assaulted my skin! No hot water?

My housemate-plumber-friend, Bill, investigated. "Donna, the hot water heater tank caught fire. You're lucky the whole house didn't burn down." I was also fortunate that the one time my hot water heater burned up, I happened to have a plumber/heating serviceman living in the house. "I'll fix it," he promised.

"Really?" I gasped, holding back tears of relief.

"Well," Bill teased, "I want to take hot showers, too, you know." He purchased a brand new water heater and installed it, even getting rid of the old one for me.

My first Christmas as a single mother arrived. After my children and I opened presents and gave each other lots of hugs, they left to spend an hour with their dad at his girlfriend's house. I relaxed on the sofa, listening to the fire crackling in the hearth and to the holiday music playing from the stereo. I didn't bother picking up the toys and wrapping paper scattered about the living room. I just sat for a while, enjoying the peaceful rest, until my stomach reminded me that the kids would soon be home for dinner.

As I stirred the turkey soup simmering on the stove, the front door opened. Naomi, Sarah, and Josh, strangely quiet, stomped up to their rooms. But four-year-old Tyler cornered me in the kitchen while I was putting away the eggnog. "Mom!" he asked in a small frightened voice, "Are you gonna have to sell the house?"

"Hmmm." My eyes narrowed in suspicion. "No. I have no plans to sell the house."

"Dad said he is gonna make you sell the house. And he and Judy are gonna buy a hot tub with the money. And we won't have enough money to live here, so we'll probably have to move off the island."

I shook my head, careful not to show how disgusted I was with his dad, "Don't you worry. We're not selling the house," I reassured him.

During the second year of our temporary divorce, my husband had trouble keeping a job and got behind on his child support payments. He also lost his license due to drunk driving, for which he was arrested more than once. Nevertheless, thanks to my new job with a raise in pay and thanks to help from family and friends, I managed to pay the bills. I was feeling stronger emotionally, too, and the children and I were doing well. Despite limited funds and all the changes we were dealing with, we shared many special times together, and I enjoyed attending their school and sports events.

One day I received a phone call from the Tisbury Board of Health. "Look out your window, Donna. What do you see?" the man on the other end said.

Watching the grey water from my broken septic system running down the street in a smelly river, I knew he wasn't calling just to be social. I scratched my head nervously and stuttered, "Oh, yeah, um, I'm trying to figure out what to do."

"Get it fixed today, or we're shutting off your water," he demanded.

I called the local septic company. The receptionist, a woman named Cheryl, who seemed to recognize my name but whom I didn't know, kindly answered my questions. I groaned when she told me how much it would cost to get my septic tank pumped. Visions of signs reading "Condemned by the Board of Health" posted on my property and of my children and I being sent to a homeless shelter flashed though my mind.

"Donna, give me your number," Cheryl interrupted my morbid musings. "I need to talk to my boss and call you back."

True to her word, Cheryl called back a few minutes later. The company cut the price in half for me and set me up on a three-year payment plan to pay off the balance. My children and I were saved from eviction, and kept the water flowing once again!

Later, when I met Cheryl in person, she told me about a dream she'd had the night before I called her office. In the dream, her brother appeared and pointed to a picture of my face and said, "Help this woman." She was amazed to discover that the woman in the dream and the one she had helped the very next day were the same person. And I was amazed at being taken care of in ways I could not have imagined.

After three years, my lawyer decided that we could risk going back to divorce court. But when we showed up to court, the divorce hearing had to be postponed once again. After reading the huge amount of money my husband owed in past-due child support and the incriminating reports of his behavior, the judge was furious. Pointing at my ex-husband, he spoke in a no-nonsense tone, "You, sir, are not leaving this room. You will go straight to jail, unless you can satisfy the terms of your divorce order."

Observing my ex-husband standing there, his hair unkempt and his clothes dusty, I almost felt sorry for him. As we all waited in shocked silence, my husband struck a bargain: He offered to turn over his half of the house to me in lieu of all the money he owed. After a brief talk with my lawyer, we agreed. The judge scheduled us to return in two months to sign the final divorce decree.

The appointed date has arrived. I am finally on my way to be officially divorced. The few seconds that pass as I approach my husband, standing at the side of the road with his thumb out, does not allow time to visit all these past memories. But they are within me, like muscle memory. The events of the last few years have shaped the woman I have become, a woman who can afford to be a little generous.

Pulling my Rodeo onto the shoulder of the road, I stop the car and lower the window. "Need a ride?" I ask.

—Donna Paulson

Silver Divorce, Golden Opportunity

"All I want is a little consideration," said Machiko, trying to keep the anger out of her voice. "And yes, love, too, and respect. Is that so ridiculous?"

"Yes," said her son Motoyuki. "Considering the fact that you are sixty-one and have been married almost forty years. Can't you hear how crazy you sound?"

Machiko took a sip of her tea and concentrated on trying to keep her hand steady. Motoyuki was her middle child, and he had always been argumentative. She had learned that sometimes it was better to simply ignore him.

"What about Dad?" said her daughter accusingly. "What's he supposed to do?"

"Your father is a resourceful man, Tami. I am sure he will find a way to cope."

Tami glared at her. "But it's not fair! He's about to retire!"

Machiko sighed and looked at her daughter. Tami was almost forty, and she had been having trouble with her own marriage. "Yes, your father is about to retire. And just think about that, if you will. He has been working hard; I don't deny that. Ten- sometimes twelve-hour days for the past forty years. But I raised three children virtually single-handedly, and you know that your father has never done a lick of housework."

"So what?" Tami said angrily.

"So what about me? Shouldn't I, too, have the chance to retire?"

Tami shrugged and shook her head, while Motoyuki rolled his eyes and sighed loudly.

"Listen," said Machiko firmly. "I've given up on your father. I'm sick of all his affairs, his boorish behavior, and his patronizing attitude. I want a divorce, and that's all there is to it."

"But at your age it's just crazy!" insisted Tami.

Machiko smiled. "Are you saying that I'm too old for romance?"

Tami frowned. "No, what I'm saying is that you're too old to be thinking of getting a divorce."

Machiko sighed. "To tell you the truth, I've been thinking about this for the past fifteen years."

Tami tried a different tack. "But, Mother, think of the shame. And your friends—think of what they will say."

"My friends?" Machiko threw her head back and laughed. "A few of them might snub me, that is true. But you do remember Fumie?"

Tami nodded. "Of course." Fumie was one of her mother's oldest friends. They had been pals since high school and had supported each other through many trials of marriage and motherhood.

"Well," continued Machiko, "Fumie and her husband have been divorced for two years. And she is currently seeing a very nice man." Machiko took a sip of her tea and raised her eyebrows at her children.

"Oh, for God's sake, Mother," said Motoyuki, exasperated.

"Your friend Fumie has money," her youngest son, Makoto, reminded her quietly. He felt like adding that Fumie was also beautiful, but he left it unsaid. Their mother was a little bullet of a woman: tough, energetic, and feisty. But you couldn't call her beautiful by any stretch of the imagination.

"Well," said Machiko, finishing her tea and picking up her purse, "money is always useful. But perhaps when your father receives his severance pay, I will be able to have my share of that. Because I have certainly earned it."

She stood up to leave and looked sadly at her three children, all glaring up at her. She loved all three of them fiercely; she really did. But she was not going to let them change her mind.

Behind her back, Machiko's children said a lot of cruel things. "She'll regret it!" insisted Tami. "A year from now she'll be begging him to let her come back." Her brothers agreed. "She thinks she's going to find romance! That is such a laugh. No man will look twice at a woman her age; it's crazy for her to think anyone will!" When they had the chance, they reminded their mother that with only forty years' experience as a homemaker, she could not possibly expect to make a living for herself. Divorce, they insisted, was not in her best interests.

But Machiko was shrewd. She waited to file for divorce until after her husband retired in order to get a share of his retirement severance payment and other benefits, including half of their household assets. That way, she explained to her exasperated children, even if she didn't find love and romance, she wouldn't starve. She found a stylish little apartment in a quiet part of Tokyo and set up housekeeping. The children seldom visited her, but once in a while they would call her.

"How's the dating going?" Tami asked her somewhat cattily on a rare visit to her mother's new apartment.

"It's a little slow," admitted Machiko, "but I love living by myself. I can eat what I want to eat when I want to eat it, and the bathroom stays just as neat as I leave it. How's your father?"

Tami sighed. "The house is a mess. And he can never find anything in it."

Machiko resisted the urge to laugh, and Tami went on.

"It's stupid, I know, but Dad didn't have the faintest idea how to use the washing machine, and he keeps ruining his acrylic sweaters."

Machiko smiled. "Give him time. He's a smart man; he'll learn."

Six months later, Tami telephoned her two brothers. Their mother, she reported, had a boyfriend. She'd been going out with him for several months and claimed it was serious. "He's obviously after her money," Motoyuki said, and her two siblings agreed.

"We'll have a chance to meet him," Tami said then. "They've invited us out for a meal."

Machiko's boyfriend turned out to be a widower exactly her age and a real charmer. He taught food science at the local university, owned his own house, and claimed that he loved to cook.

"Too good to be true," all three children concurred. "Time will tell."

They felt a little sorry for their mother, but what could they do?

"One thing's for sure," said Motoyuki angrily, "there's no way I'm going to their wedding."

A few months later, Machiko called her three children to her apartment. "I thought I should tell you that we are getting married," she said proudly.

Her three adult children stared back at her in dumb amazement.

"When?" Tami managed to get out.

"The first week of May." Machiko smiled. "Kenji is taking me to Hawaii. It will be a small ceremony, a few friends."

She didn't see the looks her children exchanged, or if she did, she had the sense to pretend she hadn't.

Machiko came back from her honeymoon with a light tan and several boxes of macadamia nut chocolates.

"No fool like an old fool," Motoyuki muttered to Makoto after their mother had left.

Tami sighed. "Boy, she is really going to regret this." Then she added wistfully, "But at least she is having a good time."

The next time Tami talked to her mother, Machiko happily reported that she and her new husband had started taking a Spanish class together.

"So how is everything then?" asked Tami guardedly.

Her mother giggled. Tami pulled the receiver away from her ear and stared at it. "If the class isn't full," she heard her mother saying, "we're thinking of signing on for ballroom dance lessons, too! Believe it or not, Kenji can already do the mambo!"

A few months later, when Machiko told Tami how much she was enjoying their dance and Spanish classes, Tami said, "I'm surprised you have time—what with that big house and the garden to look after."

Machiko smiled and shrugged. "We've got a gardener. And a lady comes to clean the house once a week."

Motoyuki stared at her. "But what about cooking? When do you have time to cook?"

Machiko laughed. "I shop. Kenji does the cooking. In fact, he's much better at it than I am. After all, he taught food science."

"Why are you studying Spanish, though?" asked Makoto, genuinely curious. "Why not English? It's much more practical."

Machiko smiled. "We're thinking about going to Spain next. We both love the idea of Spain. It's so romantic."

—Mary Whitsell

Ladies' Night

They met at Kate's house this month. Usually, a birthday or a child with a fever or a husband's being out of town kept one or two from coming, but this time everybody showed up—the three Jans, the two Debbies, Kate, and Val. Kate scooped out slabs of vanilla Häagen Dazs onto slices of black forest cake while the other women clustered around the kitchen island, forks ready, gabbing. Decaf brewed, the aroma blending with the cinnamon candle burning on the mantle, and Bonnie Raitt crooned from the living room.

Debbie R. was complaining about having to make an overnight trip each month for her wine-selling job, which was supposed to be part-time but really wasn't. They shook their heads and commiserated about the prospect of having little ones in husbands' care overnight. Things were sure to be botched. Meds missed. Faces unwashed. Diapers sagging and crooked.

Debbie W. poured another glass of merlot and didn't say much. She was a neighbor, invited because of a motherhood bond forged in front yards while her daughter and Kate's son played on blankets. Debbie hadn't gone to college like the others and sometimes felt out of place, but she smiled and nodded along, because she needed these nights, too. Only Kate knew she was having trouble with her husband. "Aren't we all," Kate had said. "Gotta weigh it out, the pluses and minuses."

Last month they'd met at Jan P.'s new house and had French silk pie and listened most of the night to Val talking about her in-laws. Nobody challenged Val, with her airline captain husband who strutted down O'Hare's terminals like a god but treated her like a slave, for the "you think you've got it bad" title. A drama teacher on hiatus, she made her mother-in-law sound like Edith Bunker: "You can't put the potatoes in the slow cooker, Val. They get all mushy. You need to learn how to make your own gravy, Val. Here, let me show you."

Sometimes, the friends all laughed so hard they became giddy—a sign of their shared desperation, Kate thought. Shedding their wife and mother skins for a few hours allowed them to breathe and to remember what it felt like to be selfish.

They tried to meet once a month on Sunday nights. It had been a year since Kate decided she needed some camaraderie and asked a couple friends to start a book club with her, not realizing it was partly their oxytocin she craved, that hormone that jumps between women and staves off depression. They got through one Sue Miller and one Toni Morrison, and then Kate's sister came and brought a friend, and by then they'd decided they didn't have time to read books and would rather talk about themselves anyway. Now, there were seven women who had twelve kids between them, and Jan P. was pregnant again.

Jan C. was thinking about having a third, too. They could afford it, with Dennis's dental practice growing. Kate and Val looked at each other wide-eyed. Ray and Tim were only's, and it was going to stay that way. *How could anyone think of two, let alone three,* Kate wondered, having spent countless evenings nodding off at the kitchen table over the last two years while Ray ran laps with the dog in the basement. Three or four hours a day of focused nurturing after a morning of teaching high school sapped her dry. As she read to Ray, book after book, she would sometimes remember her old dream of one day writing her own.

Kate loved her son wildly and would have gone to the gallows for him without a thought. But the idea that her mothering was to replace her self-ness perplexed her continually. Reading Chopin's *The Awakening* with her advanced placement English students had taken on a new poignancy that often left her speechless. There was poor Edna Pontellier, in all her 1898, tight-bodiced misery, looking for independence and fulfillment in the few small ways she was allowed, through attempts at drawing and painting, dalliances with the local men, or swims in the gulf. "What is Edna yearning for, do you think?" Kate asked her students. They were only seventeen, and to them, Edna had it made—a seaside summer resort, a nanny for the kids, and a husband who brought her bonbons. What more could a girl want?

The students read how Virginia Woolf had argued for a room of her own, and Kate heard the plea echo across time with a growing ache that the teenagers could not comprehend. "Well, at least her husband didn't beat her," Kate would joke with friends. They always laughed, even if they didn't get it.

Frankly, Kate and her husband had become nothing more than roommates. They'd been living separate lives ever since he had accused her of having a mental illness for having lost her desire for him. She clipped article after article for him to read: "Eighty percent of women report libido loss after childbirth," and "Majority of women admit the best gift a husband could give would be a weekend alone at a spa," and "Husbands' pitching in with the housework proves the most effective foreplay." He blindly clung to his belief that she was a bizarre anomaly and gave up discussing it, apparently deciding it was easier to put down rocks than tend a garden. So he plopped himself down in front of the TV and stayed there. She took care of Ray and snatched moments alone in the study, and looked forward to girls' nights.

Lately, she'd stopped looking into her own eyes in the mirror because it scared her. She felt like Greta Garbo in some old melodrama, frozen wide-eyed as the camera zoomed in on her terrible epiphanal moment: *I'm lost! Where have I gone?* The old Kate would have been amused by that image, but the current Kate wasn't and that scared her more.

She hadn't written anything besides a lesson plan or a grocery list in more than five years. She'd lost her craving to do anything the least bit creative, like sing along with Sheryl Crow on the radio or dance in the kitchen while she stirred the sloppy joes. She hardly even listened to music anymore, something that used to be such a huge part of her life. She'd starred in plays, sung at her friends' weddings, written half a book of poetry. It was as if that old self had died and a new one had stepped in—someone who was all business and all about taking care of everyone else. More and more, she had to fight the urge to jump into the car and head for the highway. Heck, just to take a walk alone in the woods would've been heaven.

Girls' night helped remind her of that old self, helped her get a tighter grasp on the rim around the chasm she was being sucked into, where she was forced to play roles she was not used to and increasingly sure she did not want. Knowing she wasn't alone with the gnawing resentments or the overloaded "mom brain"—that odd condition that makes women forget simple things like their own address or the name of the president—was at least a small comfort. Hearing her friends say that their husbands weren't much better than hers somehow helped her cope. They ate gooey desserts together and drank wine if they weren't pregnant, and they made sure to laugh hard and loud till the first one yawned, which pricked a hole in their spirits and reminded them they needed to get home.

After they had all gone, Kate was putting the cups and plates into the dishwasher when the tears came. It was not a surprise. She cried about twice a week lately, usually at night in the study after her husband had gone to bed. If it was warm outside, she would open the window to hear the rustling of wind in the trees behind the house or the hooting of their resident horned owl. His plaintive cooing felt as if it were coming from inside of her. *This can't be how I'm supposed to feel. Why didn't anyone tell me this is what it would be like?* She thought of her mother, ill and depressed most of her short life, and the one admonition she'd given to Kate and her sister: "Get a college education, so you'll never have to depend on a man." Kate had recently realized the unspoken implications of that advice. Oh, to have her mother here right now. The secrets they could share.

Kate started the dishwasher and then tidied up the family room, thinking of her girlfriends and how these monthly nights together were no longer enough. She felt the hole inside of her growing every day, the need for peace and calm, the need for balance, for artistic pursuits she longed to explore. For solitude. The moment her husband opened the garage door and stepped inside with their sleeping boy cradled in his arms, she decided it was time to call a counselor. She had to rescue her self, whether that included her husband or not. She knew it might take a long time.

A few months later, Jan P. had her third baby and had to miss a couple of girls' nights. Then Debbie R.'s husband took a job out East, and they moved away. Val started substitute teaching the next year so she could support herself once she left her husband, which she planned to do as soon as Tim turned ten. Kate's sister took a teaching job, too, so she could start a college fund for her boys. Debbie W.'s husband moved out the following winter, leaving her alone with the kids. She had to take a job at a local bank. And eventually, Kate went back to full-time teaching so she could have options. But that meant lots more papers to grade. So they cut back to meeting every other month, then twice a year. Then they just didn't meet at all anymore.

One Christmas a few years later, after her divorce, Kate got a card from Jan P. showing five smiling children, four girls and a boy, and Kate knew she would never see her again. But by then she no longer needed those escapes into girls' nights. She had a whole new world of her own.

—*Kathryn Hutchinson*

Of Mice and Men Who Aren't
There to Empty the Trap

It had been six months since the divorce. Like most divorced mothers of young children, I was sick with worry for how this failure would impact my kids. I suppose there is never a good age for a child to experience divorce, but I worried especially for my daughters, one about to hit puberty and the other a tender nine-year-old. I also feared my son, at fifteen, might feel he needed to take on the role of protector and provider.

My husband, an alcoholic, had been such a non-participant in the family that, after a month, when I sat the kids down to see how we were all doing, they all seemed fine and had not noticed any changes in their routines or lives other than the absence of "that loud snoring." Sad, I know, but that's how it played out in my situation. Still, I was on the lookout for trouble or signs of stress.

Along with the expected issues of financial pressure and exhaustion from managing the household on my own came the unexpected and quirky inconveniences, like how to deal with a rodent invasion. My only responsibility in the past had been to notify my husband that I had discovered evidence of mice. He took care of the rest.

We may as well have sent engraved invitations to all the vermin in the area—our mud room was that enticing an environment for rodents. The insulated but unfinished back entry to our country home housed bird seed and dog food as well as all the gear needed to work in the barn or play in the snow. With three active children, the coats and mittens weren't always on the hooks, and what the kids tracked in on their boots helped the room live up to its name. No wonder we were inundated every autumn with little creatures in search of a winter residence.

I'm as hospitable as the next person and have even been accused of having a Florence Nightingale complex, but when the mice began to find their way into the family living quarters and the cereal cupboard (horrors!), something had to give. Now that I was on my own, I had to step up to the plate to deal with the invasion.

Too soft-hearted to put out poison and way too squeamish to deal with emptying the remains from a trap, I borrowed a "better mousetrap." It was basically a rectangular box, a bit bigger than a shoebox, constructed of galvanized steel. It had a flat lid that slid on and off over the three chambers of the box. The bait was placed in one end, and the opposite end was the holding chamber for the caught mice, complete with plenty of holes for air and light. The center section housed the workings—a spring-wound paddlewheel. The theory was that the mouse would enter the opening in the center, searching for the bait. When the little guy tried to climb through to the bait chamber, he'd trigger the mechanism that propelled the paddlewheel to unwind one revolution, scooping him unharmed into the holding chamber. The beauty of this trap was that you could wind it up, leave it overnight, and catch several mice at a time. Of course, once they were caught, one still had to decide how to dispose of the critters.

My three children had inherited my soft-hearted, animal-loving nature and insisted the mice be released alive. I reluctantly agreed, trying not to resent my ex for not being there to fulfill his responsibility in the area of rodent control. The little bridge down the road from us had been closed, waiting for construction funds, and the children had wasted no time in staking out the unused, traffic-free portion of the road for riding their bikes and working with their 4-H goats. I decided this riverfront real estate would become the relocation turf for our caught mice. It was far enough from the house so they couldn't make their way back.

Each morning brought a moment of excitement as one or the other of my children would step out to the mud room to peer through the holes of "Come on Inn" and announce, "We've got two today," or disappointedly, "Nobody." Within a week and a half, we had apparently rounded up and relocated all the vagabonds.

Then, after a couple of quiet weeks, all the signs of little visitors began to appear again. Once more, we put fresh bait in the trap and wound it tightly before retiring.

"We caught something, but I don't know what it is!" my nine-year-old daughter, Jessica, announced with glee the next morning.

Her fifteen-year-old brother, Ben, took a quick look. "A mouse," he said, dismissing his sister's claim.

Then the middle child, Erin, peered in through the holes. "Oh, how cute!" she said. "It has a little short tail."

Now Ben showed more interest. "What? Let me look again."

Indeed, our mouse trap contained not a mouse on this morning, but a meadow vole, a relative of the hamster. Instead of the dull gray brown of the field mice we'd seen, this animal was the color of coffee with pink feet and nose.

Itching to get a better look than the little ventilation holes afforded, the kids decided to open the trap in the middle of the closed road, so they'd have a chance to observe the vole for a short time before it could scamper off into the cover of grass. I'd normally have been part of such an expedition, but I had too much to do. So down the road went my little biology lesson procession, three kids and one small rodent in a galvanized box.

Ben, being the oldest, was in charge of the release. The strategy was laid, and each child took their position, being mindful not to cast shadow on any one else's viewing area. The trap was put precisely in the center of the abandoned road, and Ben carefully slid back the top, exposing the vole, at last, to their curious eyes.

Sensing an opportunity for freedom, the vole hopped out of the trap onto the gravel. Only then did he see the three terrifying giants hovering over him as if ready to attack. There was no cover in sight—except for the relative safety of the very trap he had just been so relieved to escape. After only a second's hesitation, the vole sucked it in and dashed headlong back into the opening of the trap. Desperately looking for a hiding place, he lunged for the bait chamber . . . and triggered the device. The safety catch dropped. The spring released a shot of energy. The paddlewheel whirred.

But alas, with the lid removed, the effect was somewhat modified. Rather than being tossed safely into the holding chamber, Mr. Vole was catapulted, spinning, several feet into the air. The somersaulting rodent flew in a wide arc before landing unharmed in the lawn, drawing screams of surprise from the girls and causing Ben to jump nearly as high as the vole had flown. The initial shock passed quickly, though, and from inside the house, way up the hill, I was treated to the delightful sounds of my children's uninhibited peals of laughter.

Though I had yet to hear what was so funny, I smiled with satisfaction at their happiness and felt for the first time since their dad had left that we were going to be just fine.

—Diane Meredith Vogel

With the Passing of Seasons

I am standing in the kitchen with my work bag still slung over one shoulder, staring at the envelope sitting on the bench. On the front, in my husband's handwriting, is my name. Not the nickname he calls me, but my full name. In capitals. I know it must be serious.

Something inside doesn't want me to open it. But I do. And there it is, all in the first line: "If I didn't love you, leaving would be easy." And that's it. He is gone, and our five-year marriage is over.

The note says many other things—incidentals, like how he will be returning to retrieve his things, instructions on not to contact him, and the myriad reasons he has to leave. But I just keep looking at that first line. *He loves me*, is all I can think, knowing that if there is still love, it's not too late.

So begins my autumn, those months where everything is not yet dead but dying. For the first time in my life, I am truly alone. I wake each morning, and the first thing I do is remember The Note; then I will myself not to cry. I get up, and everything feels wrong. The house is empty, my husband is not home, and I am aching inside. At night, when I am home and sitting on the sofa, I think I hear the familiar sound of the key in the front door. My heart leaps: He's coming home! But it's my mind playing tricks. I don't know it at the time, but my husband is not coming home because he is playing Happy Family with someone else.

We met when we were teenagers; he was a singer and a national pin-up boy at the time, and I was a starry-eyed university student. Our worlds collided when we were introduced backstage at a television studio; the connection was immediate and intoxicating. We dated for three months before he proposed, and of course, I said "Yes!" Shortly after I graduated from university, we married.

We were incompatible, penniless, and hopelessly in love. We fought from the beginning and struggled through issues regarding money, lifestyle, and everything in between. Despite the differences, though, our love endured and I believed it was the glue that would always hold us together.

But suddenly after years of roller-coaster togetherness, my husband is gone. Despite his refusal to communicate, a sense of hope remains and I am convinced that if I just say or do the right thing, he will return.

Then comes the winter, those bleak months when the truth hits me hard like a frozen white bullet through the heart. Just weeks later, all sense of normalcy is gone and I am left reeling from the shock and devastation. I want answers. I want to know why. I want to know how, if he loves me, he could do this? But no matter how hard I pray for answers, none are forthcoming and my husband remains resolutely silent.

After the shock, I turn numb. Eventually, I stop crying and everything becomes robotic. It's the only way I can cope. I drive to work, and I am efficient, polite, and professional. But inside, I am dead, just a hollow shell that functions through the day, one grey lifeless foot in front of another. Every day is like this.

We had been together since I was eighteen, and now, almost a decade later, I don't know myself without him. I feel incomplete and lacking, and sometimes it seems like I am being swallowed up by the spaces, the bits that aren't there anymore. The missing him is agony; so is the knowledge that he is with someone else, despite still being married to me.

I recall the anger I'd directed toward my own parents, who I felt sure could have escaped divorce, if only they had tried harder. Suddenly, I am forced to accept the unacceptable—that sometimes it doesn't matter how hard you try; a broken marriage can happen to anyone.

Months pass, and I initiate mediation so we can settle our property. Surprisingly, it all goes smoothly. We get along like old friends, and the positive interaction between us ignites a new wave of feeling. I am overwhelmed by such a renewed sense of longing and deep feelings of loss that my father decides he will accompany me to all future meetings.

However, my husband is also affected and abruptly terminates the affair and then broaches the option of reconciliation. He declares he has always loved me and continues to do so. He confesses that he is struggling with an all-pervading sense of guilt and self-loathing, bitterly regretting the hurt and havoc he has inflicted. A teetotaler for the duration of our relationship, he admits he is now drinking to excess and suspects he is in the midst of a breakdown. He sites enormous work stress and problems within our own relationship as the reasons for his leaving. He expresses remorse over his actions and states that if we reunite it would never happen again.

I seek counsel from a well-trusted Baptist minister, who explains I am under no obligation to resume the relationship and alleviates my concern of dishonoring my marital vows if I decide not to return. It is the most difficult decision I have ever made. But when my husband and I meet up for coffee the following week, I admit that my heart has been too deeply wounded and that our marriage is beyond repair and over. We leave the café with a mutual sense of brokenness, agreeing to an amicable divorce. My husband relocates overseas, explaining that he is unable to deal with his demons and hoping that the geographical change will allow him to move forward.

Meanwhile, my winter continues for a long time, and I remain numb, cold, and lifeless. I feel nothing. Perhaps it's better that way. All my spirit, zest, and passion are gone. My smile has faded, and I am pale and skinny. I contract a virus that gets steadily worse, until, eventually, I get so sick my doctor admits me to the hospital. I am relieved. Now, someone else can take the reigns; I am just so tired of the responsibility of living. After I'm released from the hospital, I return to work, but my immune system is still so weak that I end up in the hospital again a couple of months later. My body refuses to heal, and I know it's because I have lost the will to keep going. I am losing the battle with this intolerable grief.

But then something unexpected happens. The old lady in the bed next to me dies in the night, and I am confronted with the reality that we are only here for a limited time. One day I, too, will be dead. In the meantime, what will become of me? Will I slowly fade away as she has done, or will I choose to live my best life? Despite the disappointment and fear, will I go on and do all the things I have ever wanted to?

I decide to take three months off work and to reclaim my life, my future, and my soul. I travel to Fiji with my family, and then I fly solo to Western Australia and swim with the dolphins. The divorce is finalized a few weeks after I return, and for the first time in a long time I feel glimpses of happiness. I am coming alive.

When I return home, I go back to acting school, rehire an agent, and do the work I love. I quit my office job and go freelance with my writing and acting. I decide to throw out all the remnants of the Old Life, and I leave my marital home, which we had rented for many years together. I find a new abode by the sea in a national park that provides me with the solitude and natural beauty my soul craves. Although many reminders of our time together remain and I still experience occasional twinges of sadness about what might have been, it feels wonderfully liberating to finally move on.

I celebrate spring. I start anew. I write a list of all the places I have ever wanted to travel, withdraw my savings, and go. New York, Paris, Prague, Canada—I see them all. I spend time doing my art, something I had cast aside when my marriage ended. Suddenly, I can draw again, and I am surprised at the colors flowing from my hand to the pencil and onto the page. It confirms that life is beautiful.

One day I drive through the national park and marvel at the effects of a bushfire that has swept through the greenery some time ago. I recall the burnt blackness that used to be there, the trees seemingly dead, with all hope gone. But now I am amazed the way nature regenerates with time. Lush green springs up from the black. Better yet, somehow there is even more life and richer color.

The experience of the bushfire restores something deep in my soul. I see that, after obliteration, comes greater beauty, and I start to believe that life can be better than before. Nature is never wrong, and I hold this knowledge close to my heart.

Seven years have passed since I came home to find the note on the kitchen table and thought my life had ended. I realize now that what I thought was the end was really the beginning of something more wonderful.

It is summer now, and I am living life in the sun. I am in a relationship with a magnificent man who is everything I have ever wanted and more. Life is great, and ironically, along with the contentment of coupledom, I have discovered a stronger sense of self than I've ever had before. My "independent years," as I now call them, allowed me to flourish, so that when I did meet the man of my dreams, I could be a happier significant other.

Divorce does change you. It challenges your ideals and makes you think that nothing is secure. But, in fact, you always have everything you need. Divorce teaches you many things, primarily never to take things for granted. It reinforces the need to cherish what we have while we have it and to go on afterward, even when we think we cannot. It affirms that love is a miracle and worth celebrating in whatever form it finds us, whether that be through a partner, family, friends, or the simple gift of nature.

Most of all, divorce taught me that after the cold, bleak days of winter come the renewing breezes of spring, the glorious light of summer, and the contentment of autumn.

—*V. Rachael Waters*

New Moon Rising

"Is this family court?" an attorney in a top coat asked me, the sole person sitting in the vast courtroom.

"Yes. It's a divorce grounds trial on break," I replied.

"A grounds trial? That doesn't happen!"

Well, yes it does, and it's happening to me, I thought silently. After spending eleven years too long in a psychologically abusive marriage, I was finally trying to get away—and my husband was putting me through hell. He claimed I had no grounds for the divorce I had filed for and would not divorce me. Thus, we were sitting through, at great time and expense, step one: a grounds trial.

I figured, with his hot-shot attorney and unlimited resources, I didn't have a chance. But I also knew I could no longer live in such a topsy-turvy home.

Cooking on the brand new stove and leaving behind one grain of salt could earn me an entire evening of torment, yet the man enforcing this rule refused to bathe or part with his dirty clothes. He was starting to push me around, literally. The day he finally left a bruise on me, something naive inside me shattered.

My friends were worried about me. They could see how anxious I was during the infrequent excursions my husband allowed me. My concerned neighbor pulled me aside one day to ask if I thought I might be anorexic. I couldn't begin to explain how the lump of constant tension in my throat left me unable to swallow. Even my own mother sensed there was something wrong but chose not to question me too closely. After all, I was married to a wealthy man and lived in a beautiful house; what more could I want?

It took a very perceptive girlfriend to ask me directly, "Do you want to leave?" before I, myself, realized there was a way out of this very bad decision.

It took only two hours for my friends to move me, my clothes, and my cat out. I left him a letter. My mother was kind enough to take us in. Her neighbor hid my car. And the local police were on alert if I had problems later that evening.

Breaking away was one thing. But now I would have to start a whole new life. Could I pick up the pieces of my writing career? The words I had heard daily—"old," "lazy," "worthless," "stupid"—rang in my ears. To compound this feeling, two of my three part-time jobs, both with connections to my husband, immediately evaporated. It looked like there was no end in sight to the legal shenanigans my husband could put me through. Despite my attorney's extremely fair and prudent work on my behalf, my tiny bank account—the only money to which I ever had access during the marriage—was decreasing at a rapid rate. I was sleeping in my old childhood bed, and I was scared.

One night I had a nightmare that alerted my conscious mind to just how low I had sunk. It was dark, and I was crawling through a wet, muddy gutter in front of one of my husband's rental properties. No matter how I struggled, I could not get to my feet. I was locked out, and it was taking all my energy just to continue my journey. Lifting my head, I could see the cozy apartments aglow with light above me. Looking higher, I could see thousands of white stars glittering against the navy blue velvet of the night sky. It gave me some hope.

In the morning, I rewrote my resume, rediscovering all of my good qualities as I crafted them into this document. Even at my lowest point, I had never stopped writing, having one article published nationally and finally seeing my first short story in print. I picked up my Rolodex from another time and re-contacted my friends in the journalism field to ask for references and tips on job openings.

My first job interviews were forthcoming. Although I didn't get the first job I applied for, the woman I interviewed with called me personally to tell me I came in third out of 167 people they'd tested for the position. Instead of discouraging me, this confirmed that I was of value. I was okay!

My best moment at the divorce grounds trial came when my husband's attorney asked me if I was employed. I was able to say that I was the public relations manager for the tourism department of our area's largest city. The look on my soon-to-be ex-husband's face was beyond description.

With that salary, I was able to fight as long as he cared to. I worked Saturdays and Sundays to make up for my monthly trips to divorce court. Although it took almost all of my paycheck and my mother was quite literally feeding and housing me, I won major victories that year. Not only did my ex-husband and his attorney call off the grounds trial and accept my plea for divorce, they also called off step two—a financial trial—in midstream.

When I got the call on my cell phone from my divorce attorney that they had offered a sizeable settlement, I was at a tourism conference in the warm south, staying in a luxury hotel, courtesy of my new job. That evening as I slipped from the balmy night air into the coolness of the pool, I looked up at the sliver of new moon rising against the sunset. I thought about new beginnings and remembered last year's nightmare. I realized that not only had I gotten out of the mire, I was on my way up, rising in the world just like the new moon.

—*Heidi Lux*

Dressing for Court

Straight from the pool, showered, and wrapped in a pocket-sized towel, I opened my locker and reached in: jeans, velvet shawl, cowboy boots, and a Moroccan tribal silver necklace—one of my typical casual get-ups. That's when I spotted the perfect beige, polyester skirt suit, completely absent from my wardrobe. The woman wearing it had walked into the locker room of the Boston Sports Club and now deposited her gym bag on the bench next to me. Before she could withdraw one arm from her classically cut jacket, I had obtained all the essential retail information. And in the span of a spinning class, I spun myself over to the Burlington Mall, where, in the dressing room of Casual Corner, I looked in the mirror and saw the woman I was intent on replicating.

Two days later, suited up in my slippery, unbreathable polyester skirt with matching jacket, the new conservative me stood before a white-haired, white male judge at Cambridge Probate Court. He looked at me, then he turned to my delinquent ex-husband with his long hair and hip Italian designer threads and said, "You have five minutes to pay child support, or you're going to jail."

What a surprise; he came up with $70,000.

If anyone had told me then that I would appear in three courts at least fifteen more times over the next six years with no end in sight . . .

Or that I would discover my illustrious ex-husband no longer "owned" a house, a car, a business, a condo, or perhaps a mind, because he had put it all into his new wife's name as she rose in stature from his employee to his demi-god . . .

Or that my renowned ex-husband would stand before multiple judges crying dire poverty while failing to mention how much he enjoyed the ocean view from his "wife's" new Malibu home . . .

Or that I would shell out obscene amounts of money to lawyers, burying myself in debt while my body's cells produced dangerous and deadly antidorphins . . .

Had I known all that, I may not have driven to Casual Corner that day. I might have just quietly rolled with my ex-husband's scheme to defraud me. I might have conceded that I'd never get paid for my share of the business or collect another penny of child support. Instead, I just kept going back to court, thinking that, in this outfit, with the truth on my side, this hearing will finally put an end to it.

What I discovered is that our justice system never puts an end to it. The liars keep on lying, and the lawyers keep on collecting. And, lucky for me, I have been granted the opportunity to build up a conservative subdivision in my closet—an impressive, not-at-all-me wardrobe that I will be able to wear to any court, anywhere, any season.

Down to the last detail—hair clip to shoe heel— I think I now know how to look like *everywoman*, that is the honest, earnest, plain vanilla mother who is only looking for justice. I can tell you what message a magenta scarf conveys versus the implications of a taupe scarf. I can articulate who am I with my hair up versus who I become with my hair half-up and half-down. In dozens of fashion shows in my bedroom, my girlfriends have turned into courtroom-wear consultants, nixing every item that reveals any trace of my personality—from my silk jackets to palazzo pants and wide belts. Nixed, nixed, nixed! I have learned too much about what is probably, or should be, completely unnecessary to know.

I also had the misfortune to know exactly how easy it could be for a probate court judge in his or her black robe, sitting through dizzying blitzkriegs of warring families and sifting through endless pages of motions, to miss a detail here and there—like, some guy with dimples fraudulently transferred millions of dollars of assets to his new wife. So, I keep on tinkering with the right shoes to wear with the truth in order to achieve justice. I have carted this fashion preoccupation with me everywhere, from Boston to Bali, Indonesia, from pool to pool, from hospital to hospital.

Hospital? Yes, often excluded from the waist-high pile of court records is the fact that, while the slow wheels of justice went nowhere on an incline, my very life was at stake. Yet, somehow—despite the brain hemorrhage and the brain surgery, the breast cancer and the bilateral mastectomy, the car accident and the ovarian surgery, the nerve pain and the hole in the esophagus, and, oh yes, the surgery to remove the sewing needle that waited for my foot in the shower stall of the health club—I showed up in court—appropriately dressed, of course—for doses of my ex-husband's "catastrophic poverty" routine.

And even when I wasn't sick or about to die, other important people in my life were sick and did die, including both of my parents. For a full year, I descended into my deepest, darkest grief, unable to forget that I had lawyers whose vacations I needed to fund. And when I wasn't in mourning, almost-dying, in a neck brace, on crutches, in a hospital, or in bed, one could usually find me trying to assure my devoted son of my resilience. Between the emergency room and the courtroom, he and I somehow caught the knack of enjoying ourselves.

This brings me back to dressing for court. You may be wondering how, in the midst of troubles that compare with Job's, I could even think about what to wear to court. It is a miracle, actually, that I have had the slightest will to get dressed at all. But when I clip my hair up and look instantly dignified, I feel the illusion of control over my life. And when I compose an oatmeal-and-ivory persona to step into, I occupy my brain cells with something other than death, pain, and poverty. When all is considered, including my pure love of fashion, I think I may have found the perfect obsession for me.

How I look forward to giving it up! To living the life I've fought to live. After all the depositions, motions, continuances, hearings, fruitless mediations, the long trial, the long waits for rulings, appeals, confusions, and above all, the lawyers and their shameful bills—all I want to know is: When will it end? Like most of us who simply can't afford to adjudicate injustice, I have neared the edge of surrender many times. Apparently, this is just what they want. The opposing lawyers, who amuse themselves with the mechanics of obstruction, would just love to wear me down. I ask: Can a single mother ever see the green color of justice when there are lawyers willing to fib and fudge and sanctify the hanky-panky of the deadbeat dads? Can my ex-husband's strutting, schmoozing, blown-dry lawyer keep this charade going until I finally die?

Not a chance, Mister Slick-and-Sleazy! I just might be personal friends with a force more powerful than you and your old-chum network—a fair and honorable God. This, I am trying desperately to believe.

And I am still agonizing: *Will* truth and time tell all? Will the Multimillionaire Man from Malibu, who travels the world for inspiration and enjoys the most expensive hotels and restaurants that "his wife's" money can buy, ever get his due? Will he and all the others like him ever be held responsible for the damage they do to their own children?

I would bet that this Deadbeat Dad, having submitted to a complete conscience-ectomy under the surgical command of his new wife, has probably not lost a wink of a snooze over all of this, while I, on the other hand, have agonized long past midnight and PBS's Charlie Rose for too many years. I have agonized when there were tubes up my nose and IVs in my veins. I have agonized while both of my parents lay dying.

But I have also taken action. I have written and edited legal briefs, researched rules of procedure and precedent law, played detective, and strategized as if it were my favorite competitive sport, which it is decidedly not. My smartest move of all—I packed my summer clothes in the middle of winter and flew halfway around the world to restore my bedraggled soul. Of course, for peace and pleasure that I can rely on year round, I simply imagine the outfits I will put together for my next date with the court.

At the moment, this depends on how the appeals court will rule. It could take our panel of three white male justices three months to publish their opinion, which would bring me into late winter or spring. Who knows what colors will work then? Meanwhile, I feel healthy enough now to take a few, quick, evening detours to TJ Maxx to beef up my court wardrobe with some pastel sweater sets, so not-me. Sometimes, as I swim laps or lay in bed past midnight, I ruminate: What would be the perfect outfit for the day a judge finally throws the rotten crook in jail? Something orange, perhaps?

—Donna Conrad

Driving Lessons

A gravel road, baked white in the Eastern Oregon sun, stretched ahead sixteen miles to Fish Lake, a place I'd heard about but never seen. A folding chair sat in the back of my Honda CRV, a book on the seat beside me. I was on a weekend hiking trip with friends and had asked to spend the afternoon alone. I planned to set the chair up alongside the lake, open the book, and indulge in an hour of pure pleasure.

I drove cautiously over hard-packed gravel for several miles. When a grouse popped out from behind a bush, I braked, stopped the car, and grabbed my camera. I'd never seen a grouse in the wild. Two little ones trailed her, providing a perfect start to the afternoon. My spirits, sodden from months of bitter divorce negotiations, lifted. I wouldn't celebrate when the decree was final in a few days, though I was the one who had chosen to leave. For twenty-two years I had tried to make my marriage work.

I snapped several pictures, and when the grouse family finished their careful journey, I set the camera beside my book and continued toward Fish Lake. A road branched off to my right, Dutchman Trail #1881, then another, the road to North Pine Creek. I wondered what might lie at the end of those paths but drove on toward Fish Lake and my planned respite.

I'd been equally determined to stay the course in my marriage. Once in a great while, a particularly handsome, kind, or clever man caught my eye, but I never thought about him any longer than I thought of Dutchman Trail or North Pine Creek today. I was completely focused on my relationship with my husband, Hal. A sense of failure thickened my throat. Where had I gone wrong?

The songs of a hundred birds trilling in the Ponderosa, white pines, and Aspen wafted in my open windows, brightening my heart. I approached a meadow studded with penstamon, sulfur bushwheat, and lupine, and stopped to smell the fresh air and to take more photos. Once, early in the marriage, Hal had a vase of flowers waiting on the kitchen table when I got home from a long day of teaching middle school. Feeling so exhausted I could barely walk up the short flight of stairs to our apartment, I didn't notice them immediately. When I did become aware of the fragrant, colorful bouquet, I threw my arms around Hal, but my effusive thank-you came too late, and he made his disappointment clear. In fact, he never gave me flowers again. I thought I'd been more a cheerleader than a critic over the years, but there must have been other times I'd failed to express adequate appreciation and hurt his feelings. What else?

I drove a little farther, steering carefully around several potholes. Half a dozen cows with calves wandered onto the road just ahead. One calf turned his head and looked right at me, a precious little thing, black with a white blaze covering most of his broad face. A soft lowing filled the warm air, the sound of cows and calves keeping track of each other on open grazing land. "Come here. Stay close," the mothers must be saying. Tears smarted my eyes as I thought of my three children, staying a few days with friends while I was gone. I had researched the effects of divorce on children before I left my marriage. I knew they would be all right if I gave them enough nurturing and kept communication lines open. Still, it's hard to break up a family.

I brought my mind back to the increasingly difficult task of navigating the road. It had started out as hard-packed gravel, but now loose rocks with sharp edges covered more of the surface. If I got a flat tire, I didn't have cell phone service to call AAA. My idea of a pleasant afternoon was reading a book at

Fish Lake, not reading the car manual as I learned to change a tire. So I searched carefully for the most traveled sections, where the stones were ground well into the dirt, steering right, then quickly left.

When we got engaged, Hal and I planned to live in Virginia near his job at a photo lab in Washington, D.C., after we married, and I happily left my position with Condé Nast Publishing in New York to move to Washington. I'd gone to New York filled with hope of becoming a writer, and I'd made some good connections with fellow writers and editors. But D.C. was close enough to keep up those connections. The New York scene paled beside the promise of marriage to my witty, multitalented boyfriend. How easily I gave up my writing dreams to be with him. At that time, our course seemed to consider both our needs. I couldn't see how rough the road would become.

When we headed west to meet each other's families, an old friend in Los Angeles looked at Hal's portfolio and offered him freelance work doing advertising. Hal was thrilled. I cried. I had been raised in Los Angeles and had been looking forward to living on the East Coast. Plus, my writing contacts would be three thousand miles away. Still, I never questioned putting his wishes first. That's what a good wife would do, I thought. Writers could write anywhere. Looking back, I wonder if it was then I should have pulled out a map and asked to rethink our direction. We were both young and eager to please. We might have been able to negotiate a different way.

We moved to Los Angeles, where Hal soon learned that the promise of freelance work carried no real intention and that to compete in the world of freelance photography he needed to return to school. So I put away my notepads, got a provisional teaching certificate while I went to school for the real thing, and started to teach. Both my parents had been teachers, and I recognized the social value of their profession, but I wanted to write. We agreed that when Hal graduated from Los Angeles Art Center, it would be my turn to pursue my interests.

When Hal graduated, I told him I wanted to do more postgraduate work at a school in Florida. We had a baby then, and I was working part-time as a research assistant while I got my master's. We would be there just a few years, I promised, and then he could set up a studio in a place of his choice.

"You must be kidding," he said. "Who's going to take care of Tami? We can't just take off."

A picture of that moment pops into my mind as I take a hard left around an enormous pothole.

Our relationship grew more and more strained. We had three children and found our values often differed on how to raise them. Our voices grew louder, our laughter more rare. The road we tried to travel together grew so littered with sharp rocks that I could barely find a way to move forward. Still, I thought if I stayed alert and drove carefully, I could make it.

My stomach is sick with the pain of my memories. I'm creeping now toward Fish Lake. I've seen potholes on a few of the back roads in Portland, but none the size of these. And never gravel this size. I look at my odometer. Five miles down, eleven to go. Should I turn back?

I stop the car and walk forward on the road, seeing if it gets better farther on. After five minutes, it hasn't smoothed out at all. I look at my watch. Returning, the sun will be behind me, shading the potholes.

I had spent the last year, at least, in the dark shadow of depression. Only those who have experienced it can understand the kind of mental and emotional pain it brings. Once I recognized the symptoms in myself, I saw them in my children as well. The road simply got impassable.

Gravel crunched as I backed my car and turned around, away from Fish Lake, toward my friends and the smooth highway. And I forgave myself, a little, for being unable to make my marriage work. The serenity I'd hoped to find at the lake I would some day find in myself.

—*Samantha Ducloux Waltz*

Getting Rid of the Drek

I lifted the lid on the old twenty-gallon steel can and tossed in a manila envelope. The garbage can never made it to the curb on trash day. Instead, it had long served as a sort of circular file for an accumulation of legal documents that could feed a fire for hours. At the bottom was a protection from abuse petition, on top, the final divorce decree. In between was the chronological record of three contentious years in divorce court. I wanted to cry every time I looked at it.

"*Genug es genug!*" (Enough is enough!) My mother did not mince words.

Both of my parents had stood behind me through all the hostilities, but Mom was tired of watching me beat myself up. She told me time after time, "Enough is enough." But I couldn't move on. I'd been married nine years, and I had to know where I'd failed. Of course it was my all my fault; my ex-husband had said so. I replayed every argument and reread every court transcript until I thought I was losing my mind.

When I met Sam, I thought he was perfect: intelligent, nice-looking, and a go-getter. There were a few red flags, but I didn't recognize them. One night I dated another man, and Sam called the house fifteen times while I was out. Dad thought he was a stalker. I was flattered and laughed it off. When Sam disparaged his parents, I was sympathetic and pleased he could confide in me.

We married after dating only six months, and I became pregnant immediately. When our daughter was born, we were ecstatic. I was determined to be the best wife and mother I could be.

Hannah was three months old when Sam suggested I go back to work. I was surprised but agreed. We were house-hunting and could use the extra money. I was fortunate to find a part-time job near home, and two years later we added a son to our family.

Sam and I both wanted more kids, but I thought we should wait a few years. In addition to caring for two babies and a new house, I was working part-time again. But Sam was convinced our children should be close in age, and he wanted them all before he was thirty. When he made up his mind about something, he was relentless. It was easier to give in than to argue with him. We had another beautiful boy.

Sam loved to brag about his three children, but he rarely spent time with them. We saw him less and less. If he wasn't working, he was at a sporting event. I made excuses for him: He worked hard; he needed an outlet.

Meanwhile, I was busier than ever. Yet, Sam always seemed to find fault with me. I fell short in every way—incompetent, unappreciative, a social embarrassment, an inadequate parent—and he constantly let me know he deserved better. My self-esteem reached an all-time low. I didn't know who I was any more.

Sam had a small office in the basement. One day he caught me using the phone on his desk. He was furious. His reaction seemed out of proportion. Was he hiding something?

Before long, I was playing detective, and I discovered a side of Sam I'd known nothing about. In his desk I found bottles of pain killers and tranquilizers along with receipts from gambling casinos and a letter from a strange woman.

I confronted him, and he agreed to see a marriage counselor. Sam treated our sessions as a joke. He told the therapist, "I am who I am. I'm not going to change."

Still, I was shocked when he asked for my engagement ring. He'd been caught forging checks and needed money to pay back his clients. Afraid he would lose his job, I allowed him to sell my ring.

I balked, though, when he insisted I sign papers to mortgage our house. Sam wasn't used to opposition, and we had our worst fight ever. He struck me, and I got a restraining order. The rest is history.

My part-time job paid for groceries, and my parents took on the mortgage and utilities. I felt worthless, and was afraid to look for a full-time job. It was my dad who convinced me to take a civil service exam. I was stunned when I passed and even more surprised when I was called to interview for an engineering aide position.

I reported to an office on the fifth floor of the municipal building. A large man sat smoking behind an old wooden desk that took up half the room. The stench of stale cigarette butts permeated the small space. He looked up and scrutinized me. His expression said it all, and he wasn't happy with what he saw. It didn't surprise me. I wasn't happy with me, either. I was so nervous my silk shirt stuck to my ribs. *Please, God, don't let there be wet spots under my armpits.*

The man motioned me to a seat.

"I'm the chief surveyor. You scored pretty high on the test. Are you familiar with survey work?"

I froze. *Should I bluff or be truthful and tell him I have no clue?*

Whump whump whump. The hypnotic beat of an ancient floor fan ticked off the seconds as the manager tapped a pencil on the desk, waiting for my answer.

"Do you know what a surveyor does?" he finally asked.

"Uh . . . calls people on the phone and asks them questions?"

He sighed.

"We do construction surveying. My men provide locations for water and sewer pipes."

Huh?

"Would you be willing to climb down a manhole, knowing you might encounter rats or toxic fumes?"

When hell freezes over. "No problem."

"I see you have children. Is that going to be a problem?"

Is he kidding? "Oh, no; I have an excellent baby-sitter." *Do I? It doesn't matter. I won't get the job.*

"Okay, go get your physical."

There was a moment of stunned silence.

"I'm hired?" I stammered.

"If you pass the physical. Oh, and dress casual; you'll be working outside."

I pushed down an uneasy feeling. *Was I the token female? Would the men accept me or would they think I was unqualified?*

The first day on the job I was scared to death, but at least I wasn't the only woman. There was a secretary, a timekeeper, and another female engineering aide. But there were also forty-six men in hard hats and work boots. Some women might think they were in heaven in that situation, but I didn't.

The chief took me on a tour of the building. " . . . and this is the drafting room."

Now I was in heaven—surrounded by drafting tables, drawing boards, pens, ink, and triangles. I'd had some art classes and knew something about drafting. My hands itched to grab a pencil.

"I'd like to draft," I blurted out and immediately tensed, waiting for his put-down.

"We have a big backlog. Let's see what you can do."

I couldn't believe he was going to give me a chance.

The day I earned a place in the drafting room was the day I realized I'd been wrong to judge all men by my ex-husband. And I'd been wrong to let Sam's judgment determine what I could and couldn't do. I broke through the wall of self-doubt I'd been living behind and opened myself to the possibility of accomplishment. That day, I realized I could build on my skills and provide for myself and my children.

My mother had been right. There was nothing to be gained from analyzing the past. It was time to look ahead. It was time to put out the trash.

—*Gail Pruszkowski*

A Love Letter to My Ex

Now, don't get me wrong. I'm not one of those "Oh, we're divorced, but let's be pals and all celebrate major holidays together, la di da" kind of fools. For the longest time after my second (!) divorce, whenever anyone told me I should be charitable toward my ex, I would say: "Sorry, I'm old-fashioned, I believe in hating my ex-husbands."

It was a rule I followed religiously. My second ex (who can even remember the first?) had done so much against me that I felt obliged to hate him for all eternity. It was a matter of pride—or so I thought at the time. In truth, of course, there was much Sturm und Drang on both sides. Ours had always been a passionate association, for better or worse . . . until a protracted, financially and emotionally devastating legal battle did us part.

After I left him and fled three thousand miles with our son, my ex married a tall blonde named Pauline. I am a tall blonde named Paula. You and I may readily see the Freudian implications here—but he did not. I would have thought it hilarious, a back-handed compliment of ironic proportions, if I hadn't been so pissed off. How dare he get on with his life with another blonde with (half of) my name! How dare he be happy with half-name Pauline! How dare he be happy with anyone besides me, even women whose first names did not begin with P! No surprise to you, I was delighted that it didn't work out. It took seven years, but blessed with a killer instinct I did not possess, my Döppelganger eventually brought my ex to his knees. "Karma!" I told anyone who would listen, "Karma in my lifetime!"

Naturally, I had my own share of dalliances during this time, but whenever any man had grown fond enough of me to ask me to marry him, I'd back away, saying, "No thanks. My second husband cured me of marriage." That was my story, and I was sticking to it.

I did stick to it—and broke at least three very nice men's hearts in the process. When I finally decided eight years after my divorce that I was ready to make a commitment, I couldn't find anyone I liked. I dated a number of perfectly suitable, attractive, gainfully employed, age-appropriate guys with good credit histories who should have turned me on and God knows pulled out all the stops to do just that. Some even had all their hair. I was fifty-one, for goodness sake, in no position to be so picky, but still I demurred. I was waiting for that twist in your gut, the one you can't resist even when you know better. The one that I'd always felt with my ex. And admittedly still did, nearly a decade later, although now I believed it was the pull of anxiety, not attraction.

Life is full of surprises: layoffs, earthquakes, divorce. I hate surprises. I spent my postdivorce years avoiding surprises, abandoning life in disaster-prone California to live in historic, stable New England, where the seasons pass with a predictable rhythm that I found profoundly reassuring. Boring, even. But safe.

Yet, no matter how you try to safeguard yourself against life's little aftershocks, the earth still moves under your feet when you least expect it. For me, it all started with a teenager, always an upset waiting to happen. My fifteen-year-old son wanted an extravagantly expensive electronic toy for Christmas. I wanted to give it to him, but couldn't quite pull it off on my own. So I swallowed my pride and contacted my ex to see if we could get it for our son together. I called, and the man who usually answered, "Oh, if it isn't the bitter divorcée," instead said, "Hi." A modest start, to be sure, but that little "Hi" led to "How are you," which led to—shocker of all shockers—"I'm sorry."

I'm sorry? My ex was apologizing? To me? I was stunned. More impressive, I was speechless.

Since I couldn't speak, he did. He talked a long time, and I listened—each an unprecedented act, respectively.

"I'm sorry, too," I whispered.

"What?"

"You heard me," I said, and hung up. Well, you didn't expect me to belabor the point, did you?

That was the first of many such conversations. Our son got his present, and we got closure. We even went to lunch together, the three of us, the day after Christmas. The last time my ex and I had been in the same room together was in court. That lunch was the only civilized meal our son ever remembers us sharing together. We made a new memory for us all that day.

If you're now waiting for me to say that we all lived happily ever after, get over yourself. This is a divorce story. That said, upon seeing my ex after all those years, I got that telltale little tug in my gut for the first time in nearly a decade.

La di da.

—*Paula Munier*

Don't Ride the Clutch

Everything hurt, right up to the hairs on my head. The best place to pitch a tent, someone said, was where scorpions didn't nest, because they'd come back if I shooed them away. My aching body told me I should have picked some place other than a mound of granite bigger than my living room.

I cracked open an eyelid. Through the flap of my tent, I saw Ponderosa pines silhouetted in the cool light of the moon. Their lanky shadows stretched across a clearing dusted in tones of gray velvet. Way too early to get up.

Kneading my jacket into a pillow, I squirmed into a new position and discovered that sometime during the night my air mattress had taken the easy way out. The only thing between me and the rock of ages was one inch of Dacron filling in my sleeping bag.

What was I thinking? The question was rhetorical. I knew what was going on.

Divorced for fifteen years and the mother of two grown sons, I was in the throes of a raging midlife crisis. Starting college at thirty-seven, earning two degrees, and climbing a corporate ladder wasn't cutting it. I still felt like someone's castoff. I wanted—no, I needed—to up the ante on my life's experience, move from dimpling the surface like a water spider to having a salmon-like go at that last desperate swim upstream to deposit some imaginary legacy before I turned red and died.

So here I was, so far out of my comfort zone I was off the map. I, a white-collar manager, had volunteered to drive a Jeep Jamboree and write about it for the company newspaper. I joined 160 men and women who cranked their engines to life on a Friday morning and rolled out of Georgetown, California, like a column of mechanized ants. We were headed for Lake Tahoe via the Rubicon Trail in the Devil's Playground of the Sierra Mountains.

On a scale of one to ten, the Rubicon is a difficult ten, but I was in decent shape. I took aerobics classes. I lifted free weights. I'd spent weeks hiking around my neighborhood. I hadn't practiced sleeping on granite.

I had been assigned to share the driving of one of the vehicles with the jamboree consultant and two professional journalists. The four of us piled into a stick-shift Jeep Wrangler that had a protective skid plate mounted under the engine's vital organs. The doors had been removed for safe keeping and the hardtop replaced with a square of canvas some quick wit had named a "bikini top." The Wrangler was loaded with camping gear and survival equipment. I naively ignored the not-so-subtle warnings: "protective skid plate," "safe keeping," "survival equipment."

While driving sixty miles per hour on the highway to the trailhead on Friday, we'd shouted at each other over the roar of the wind, the snap of the bikini, and the whine of the tires pounding the asphalt. I watched the pavement race past under my right elbow and kept a two-handed, white-knuckled grip on my seat belt. Just before we entered the trail, the consultant handed out the "Off-Road Driving Instructions."

"Use low gear."

"Be sure your hubs are engaged."

"Start the vehicle in gear, without the clutch." (I thought manual transmissions *had* to be clutched.)

"Idle over rough spots going uphill."

"Keep your foot off the clutch. If your tires start to spin, give it more throttle, never clutch."

"Use compression going downhill; touch the brake only as needed; don't clutch."

"Don't straddle boulders. Do straddle ruts."

"Don't ride the clutch."

"Buckle your seat belt."

The instructions bore a close resemblance to "Damn the torpedoes. Full speed ahead," but I wasn't worried. This was the adventure I was looking for. Besides, we had only nine miles to cover the first day. How bad could it be?

After a half-hour of brain-jarring travel over tree branches and through deep ruts that skirted huge pine trees, I began to reconsider my need to bring excitement into my life. Then we got into the nitty-gritty of the Rubicon. We suffered high-altitude stalls, usually with at least one wheel hanging over empty space. We "walked" up fifty-foot-high granite slabs at virtually right angles to the world. We bounced and slid down rock-laden sluices. I watched open-mouthed as the Jeep ahead of us took a rolling tumble when the driver miscalculated. Not to worry. Before the dust settled, the helping hands of a support team righted the vehicle and sent it on its way.

It took six hours to travel the first nine miles of the Rubicon.

After a quick dip in a frigid mountain stream and a plate of something to eat—I don't remember what—I wriggled my tired bones into a sleeping bag and closed my eyes at the same time daylight abandoned the mountains.

When the sun aimed its first golden rays in the direction of the mess tent, I kicked aside the remains of the deflated air mattress, stuffed a handful of aspirin into my pocket, and crawled out of the tent like an arthritic spider. My hairstyle was vaguely reminiscent of a rat's nest, so I pushed it under a baseball cap and shuffled over for some high-octane caffeine. Along the way, I checked out my fellow campers spread across several acres.

They all shared a passion for off-roading, and all were driving some version of every small Jeep sport utility vehicle manufactured since World War II. But in their other lives, they were mechanics, engineers, doctors, students, and writers. A conga line of SUVs snaked around the mechanics' corral, waiting to repair burned-out clutches. It was comforting to know that I wasn't the only one out of her urban element.

Gratefully, I learned we would spend Saturday recovering from all that fun of the day before. Then I discovered that recovery did not include rest.

I declined the opportunity to spin rooster tails out of a mud pit and opted out of rubber tubing in a stream fed by melting snow. To solidify my credentials as a genuine four-wheeler, I did agree to test my mettle driving a course of corrugated roads. Since that meant keeping all four tires on solid ground, I thought, how bad could it be? Sigh. The roads turned out to be little more than former animal tracks that often rose to the crest of steep inclines and then disappeared from view. Moving forward required an act of faith.

The next morning we started out of the Sierras, headed for Lake Tahoe. The Wrangler crawled through wet, rock-strewn notches carved between boulders. It muscled its way over bulging pine tree roots bracketed in front and behind by washouts.

As the only woman among three men, I will be eternally thankful I wasn't driving when the Jeep straddled a boulder and came to a rocking halt. Some nameless someone had high-centered the Wrangler, leaving all four wheels spinning in air. After we leaned against the front fender to push the skid plate off the boulder so that at least one tire could touch the ground, the Jeep crawled out of trouble. We spent our last few hours in the Sierras climbing a two-track road until we paused atop a scarp.

Before me was an awesome alpine cathedral: piney woods for walls, lush meadows for carpets, and the firmament for its roof—a scene that soothed every ache, bruise, and broken fingernail.

I'd crossed the Rubicon. I'd reached the mountain top.

Like a switch being turned on, my brain made the connection. Traversing the Rubicon Trail was a perfect analogy for my life. The divorce I didn't want wasn't an insurmountable failure. I kept going forward, even when I had to navigate seemingly impossible obstacles. I stepped out on faith when I couldn't see what was waiting for me down the road. I did much more than survive my divorce: I succeeded.

Every so often, when I find myself struggling through a period of divorced-woman's angst, I think about the rules for off-roading: idle over the rough spots going uphill. If your wheels start to spin, give it more throttle. Don't ride the clutch. Buckle your seat belt.

Unlike the Rubicon Trail, life doesn't come with such a clear set of instructions. Those four lines simply remind me that I can make it over the rough spots if I just keep going, taking things one step at a time. And I know I'd better buckle up because it's going to be a bumpy ride. More important, I know that, like that bloody determined salmon, I can leave no more perfect legacy than my children and my love for them. Everything else is temporary.

—C. J. Petterson

Contributors

Linda Clare ("For the Birds") is the author of three nonfiction books and many award-winning short stories, essays, and articles. She lives in Oregon with her husband and teaches writing at the college level. She's busy helping her mom adjust to single life, with a clock that's still off by one bird.

Donna Conrad ("Dressing for Court"), who resides in Massachusetts, has won several awards for her children's book, *See You Soon Moon*, as well as several awards from several divorce courts. Her essays and short stories appear frequently in literary journals. The founder of College Bound Essays, she helps students discover and craft their college essays. She also designs clothing, but never for court.

J. M. Cornwell ("Lullaby and Goodbye") is a writer who lives in Colorado, where she now sings lullabies to the birds and neighbors. Her stories appear in *Chicken Soup® for the Adopted Soul*, *A Cup of Comfort® for Single Mothers*, and *Haunted Encounters*. She is also a licensed "Extra" amateur radio operator.

Lana Dalberg ("A Clean Heart") lives with her two daughters in the San Francisco Bay Area and works as a grant writer. Her articles have appeared in *Switchback*, *Your Stepfamily Magazine*, *True Words from Real Women*, and *Story Circle Journal*.

Sylvia M. DeSantis ("Isn't That Special") resides in Pennsylvania, where she teaches, writes, and develops Interaction Design. Her work has appeared in the *Chicken Soup for the Soul®* series, Harvard University's African American National Biography project, and Summer Shorts. She has just completed a middle-grade novel, *The Lost Hart of Cape May: A Veruca Silver Mystery*.

Jocelyn Duval ("Something in Common") is the pen name of a businesswoman, who uses her writing and editing abilities in a family business in Kansas City. Recently, she tossed aside press releases, ad copy, and executive summaries to pursue two long-time dreams: writing short stories and teaching. Even more than writing, she enjoys her children and her grandchildren.

Carole Fowkes ("First You Cry") is a registered nurse who also holds a B.A. in communication. She currently works as a clinical trainer. Originally from Cleveland, Ohio, she has lived in Tampa, Florida, and the Chicago area, but admits that her heart belongs to the Lone Star State. She currently resides in Plano, Texas.

Marilyn A. Gelman ("New Year's Resolution") lives in Fair Lawn, New Jersey. A writer and editor, she also advocates for people living with mild traumatic brain injury and other invisible disabilities. Her publication credits include the *New York Times, Creative Nonfiction, A Cup of Comfort® for Dog Lovers,* and *True Confessions.*

Nancy George ("Answering the Dreaded Question: Are You Dating Anyone?") is a university editor and freelance writer in Richardson, Texas. Her work has been published in numerous publications, including *Angels on Earth,* the *Christian Science Monitor,* the *Dallas Morning News,* and *Bark Magazine.* She is the proud parent of a daughter and two sons.

Elizabeth King Gerlach ("The Cheese Stands Alone") is the author of two award-winning books, *Just This Side of Normal* and *Autism Treatment Guide* (Future Horizons). Elizabeth and her ex-husband remained friends and co-parented two great boys. After standing alone for eight years, she remarried and lives with her husband, Scott, in Eugene, Oregon.

Faye "Sunny" Glessner ("A Potato Epiphany") lives happily in Port Hueneme, California. As a Navy brat, she lived across the United States; as an adult, she has traveled around the world. She loves being a grandparent, treasures the fine friends she has made, and aspires to be a writer when she grows up.

Eileen Clemens Granfors ("Bruised but Not Broken") of Santa Clarita, California, retired from teaching to travel, kayak, and write. She credits UCLA's Writers' Program for giving her the confidence to go public with her memoirs, poetry, and fiction. She is eager to move to the Ozarks, where she and her husband own their dream house.

Ona Gritz ("The Stepfather Question") lives in Hoboken, New Jersey. She writes a monthly column for the online journal *Literary Mama*. Her second book for children, *Tangerines and Tea: My Grandparents and Me*, was named Best Alphabet Book of 2005 by *Nick Jr. Family Magazine*. Her essays and prize-winning poetry have been published in numerous journals and anthologies.

Tisha R. Harris ("Guess Who's Coming to Dinner") is a freelance writer and tele-fundraiser residing in Southern Oregon. She enjoys writing heartwarming personal-experience essays and specializes in writing for children. Her work has appeared in *Highlights for Children, Boys' Quest,* and *Fandangle* magazines. When not writing, she enjoys the outdoors with her family.

Cynthia Harrison ("Snow Day") lives in Michigan with her husband of twenty-three years. She teaches writing at Macomb Community College, using *Your Words, Your Story,* her creative-writing memoir disguised as an instruction manual. Since 2002, she has written almost daily about the writing process on her blog, "A Writer's Diary."

Janet Baker Hayhurst ("On the Road to Redemption") writes fiction and nonfiction in Guadalajara, Mexico, because it is as far as her resources will take her from Pittsburgh's divorce industry. In San Atanasio parish, staffed by priests from the faithful Fraternity of St. Pius X, she enjoys traditional mass and Catholic culture, and heals.

Jodi Henry ("Just Fine") is a writer and editor living in Eugene, Oregon. She has won several writing contests, and her work has appeared in various publications, including the 2006 Oregon Writer's Colony anthology and the Women on Writing (WOW) web site. She is currently working on a collection of personal essays.

Jane Ann Hiteshew Holland ("What I Know Now") lives on a two hundred-acre farm in Walkersville, West Virginia, with her two youngest children, Matthew and William, six cats, ten dogs, and fifty cows. Her three older children are attending West Virginia University. She is continuing her education in business and finance, hoping to start her own business showing other displaced wives how to survive and prosper financially and emotionally after divorce.

Amy Houts ("Honeymoon for Four") lives in Maryville, Missouri. She is the author of twenty-four books for children. Her recent cookbook for children, *Cooking Around the Country with Kids*, explores American regional food. She also is an instructor for the Institute of Children's Literature, teaching the correspondence course, "Writing for Children and Teenagers."

Kathryn Hutchinson ("Ladies' Night") teaches English and is a fine arts coordinator at a large high school near Chicago. Still happily single, she often dreams of an alternative reality where she could pursue a career as a writer or singer. Kate's teenage son, who has autism, has been the inspiration for much of her writing.

Elaine Greensmith Jordan ("Burned"), a former teacher and minister, now lives in Arizona, where she writes essays, sings in a choir, and contemplates the past. She remarried, was widowed, and has remarried again. The lessons learned from the first marriage, told in this story, have served her well.

Jolie Kanat ("Like a Horse and Carriage"), of Marin County, California, is a writer of every medium. Her credits include a nonfiction book, *Bittersweet Baby*; a column for the San Francisco Chronicle; "Perspectives" essays for National Public Radio, songs for Time Warner and Universal Studios productions, two CDs for children with special needs, and greeting cards for Schurmann Fine Papers.

Cathi LaMarche ("Thief of Hearts") is the author of the novel *While the Daffodils Danced*. While busy at work on her second novel, she is also pursuing her master's degree in teaching. She resides in Missouri with her husband and her two children.

Karen Leland ("My Second First Date with My Spouse") is president of Sterling Consulting Group and the author of *Watercooler Wisdom: How Smart*

People Prosper in the Face of Conflict, Pressure and Change. In her spare time, she writes freelance, paints, and sings. She lives in Marin County, California, with her second husband, Jon.

Tina Lincer ("Dating Redux and Other Cosmic Jokes) is a writer in Upstate New York. Her features and humor essays have been published in local and national newspapers and magazines, National Public Radio online, and anthologies. She's a good sport about being the butt of cosmic jokes.

Adrienne Lindholm ("The Long Thaw") lives in Anchorage, Alaska, where she works for the National Park Service. Though she spends most of her free time exploring the wild mountains and rivers of the North, she has given up on winter camping.

Heidi Lux ("New Moon Rising"), a native of Rochester, New York, lives with her second-time's-the-charm husband in Saxony, Germany, where she works as an English instructor. Her publishing credits include *Transitions Abroad* and *German Life* magazines, *StyleCenturyMagazine* online, *Antique Week* and the *NY-PA Collector* newspapers, and *A Cup of Comfort® for Families Touched by Alzheimer's*.

Donna Miesbach ("It's About Love") is a certified meditation and yoga instructor and spirituality workshop leader in Omaha, Nebraska. Her articles and poems have appeared in *Unity Magazine, Daily Word, Chicken Soup® for the Teenage Soul II,* and *Ideals.* Her program Tools for Teens is used throughout the United States and abroad.

Barbara Mountjoy ("Under the Big Top") has been a published writer for more than thirty years and has raised seven children. She still keeps her day job as a family law attorney and her night job as mother to three special-needs children, and tries to mind an absent-minded, computer-geek husband as she's writing.

Paula Munier ("A Love Letter to My Ex"), veteran writer and editor, is the author of *On Being Blonde* and the young adult novel *Emerald's Desire.* Her short stories have appeared in such anthologies as *A Cup of Comfort® for Writers, Raging Gracefully, Letters to My Teacher, HerStory, Angel Over My Shoulder, Tour of Duty,* and *Horse Crazy.* The mother of three, she now lives south of Boston in a lakeside cottage with her family, two dogs, and a cat.

Donna Paulson ("I'll Take the High Road") lives with her four children on Martha's Vineyard, an island in Massachusetts. She enjoys being an office assistant for a landscape company, which allows time for her writing. She credits her faith and her sense of humor for helping her to survive life as a single mother.

C. J. Petterson ("Don't Ride the Clutch") is the pen name of Marilyn Johnston, who retired from her career in Detroit's automotive industry and is now living and writing in Mobile, Alabama. She is a charter member of the Mobile Writers' Guild and is in the process of completing her second novel.

Gail Pruszkowski ("Getting Rid of the Drek") is a lifelong resident of Philadelphia, Pennsylvania. She works as a drafting supervisor while pursuing her love of reading, writing, and reviewing for *Romantic Times BOOKreviews* magazine. She shares her life with three children, five grandchildren, two Tonkinese cats, and one patient husband.

Darcy Purinton ("Roadside Assistance") is a freelance writer who lives in Windsor, Connecticut, where she works as an English teacher and dean at the Watkinson School. Her two children and her love of Vermont fill her life with the energy necessary to survive life's fiercest trials, even divorce.

S. Ann Robinson ("Geronimo!") enjoyed four decades as an instructor, business manager, seminar leader, staff writer, wife, and mother. She now lives in Northern Virginia, where she teaches at the local community college, attends American Sign Language classes, writes for regional publications, and enjoys nurturing her granddaughter, Victoria.

Elizabeth Sellars ("Can I Have My Town Back?") was born in Seattle, Washington. She received a B.A. at Hollins University in Virginia and an M.A. in Spanish at the University of Virginia. She now lives in Ajijic, Jalisco, Mexico, where she teaches English.

Sheila Smith ("Smithing My Life") lives in Corvallis, Oregon, where she writes, trains dogs, and serves as a Unitarian Universalist lay minister. Some of her sermons and published articles show how positive dog training relates to the meaning of life.

Anne-Christine Strugnell ("Can't Stop the Ocean" and "The Passage"), who sometimes writes as Meridian James, is a professional writer and amateur mother living in Marin County, California. Her work has been published in *A Cup of Comfort® for Writers* and in magazines serving the high-tech industry and has aired on National Public Radio.

Natalie Sullivan ("Happy Father's Day, Mommy") grew up in Panama City, Florida. Her best hours are spent writing, drawing, acting, and raising her daughter, Rose. She resides with Rose in Tampa, Florida, where she works as a receptionist for an engineering firm.

Barbara Neal Varma ("Playing with Fire" and "We Meet Again") turned to journaling during her divorce. Though the marriage ended, the writing continued, evolving into a freelance writing career that has produced several award-winning essays. Now happily remarried, she lives in Southern California.

Diane Meredith Vogel ("Of Mice and Men Who Aren't There to Empty the Trap") lives in rural mid-Michigan. Her children are grown and on their own now. Her stories have appeared in four other *Cup of Comfort*® books. Along with writing, Diane enjoys projects around the home, gardening, and canoeing. She is currently marketing a novel.

Samantha Ducloux Waltz ("Driving Lessons") is an award-winning freelance writer in Portland, Oregon. Her essays can be seen in the *Cup of Comfort*® and *Chicken Soup*® series and a number of other anthologies. She has also published adult nonfiction and juvenile fiction under the names Samantha Ducloux and Samellyn Wood.

Tanya T. Warrington ("When the Rubber Band Breaks") is a freelance writer who has published articles, devotionals, and poetry. It brings her joy to encourage other divorced women and to empower others to live God's gift of abundant life.

V. Rachael Waters ("With the Passing of Seasons") is an Australian writer and artist who divides her time between various seaside abodes. She loves the ocean, Matisse, writing, drawings, and "going the other way." She is inspired by all those brave enough to live their dreams.

Mary Whitsell ("Silver Divorce, Golden Opportunity") is an expatriate American who lives in Scotland with her family and enjoys writing for both young people and adults. She is currently writing a memoir about the decades she has spent learning Japanese and living in Japan.

Renea Winchester ("With This Ring") is a writer who splits her time between Western North Carolina and Atlanta, Georgia, where she resides with her family and a labradoodle named Charlie. She writes fiction and nonfiction. Her work received the Appalachian Writers Association Award and has appeared in *Birds and Blooms*.

Amy E. Zajac ("That Magic Moment") lives in Calhoun, Georgia, sharing her home with her elderly parents and working for a major consulting company. She writes part-time about her two daughters, now grown, and her life's experiences. Currently, she is working on her first novel.

About the Editor

Colleen Sell has compiled and edited twenty-five volumes of the *Cup of Comfort*® book series. A veteran writer and editor, she has authored, ghostwritten, or edited more than a hundred books; published scores of magazine articles and essays; and served as editor-in-chief of two award-winning consumer magazines, associate editor of a business magazine, and home and garden columnist of a newsmagazine. She shares her life and an old farmhouse on a forty-acre farm-in-the-making in the Pacific Northwest with T. N. Trudeau—living proof that the third time really is a charm.